MARVEL

MARVEL AGE OF COMICS

AF752410

MARVEL SUPER HEROES SECRET WARS: THE EPIC 1980s SAGA

AN EXPLORATION BY

TOM K. MASON

BLOOMSBURY ACADEMIC
NEW YORK • LONDON • OXFORD • NEW DELHI • SYDNEY

BLOOMSBURY ACADEMIC
Bloomsbury Publishing Inc, 1359 Broadway, New York, NY 10018, USA
Bloomsbury Publishing Plc, 50 Bedford Square, London, WC1B 3DP, UK
Bloomsbury Publishing Ireland, 29 Earlsfort Terrace, Dublin 2, D02 AY28, Ireland

BLOOMSBURY, BLOOMSBURY ACADEMIC and the Diana logo are trademarks of Bloomsbury Publishing Plc

MARVEL PUBLISHING
Jeff Youngquist, VP, Production and Special Projects
Brian Overton, Manager, Special Projects
Sarah Singer, Editor, Special Projects
Jeremy West, Manager, Licensed Publishing
Sven Larsen, VP, Business Development and Licensed Publishing
David Gabriel, VP, Comic Sales and Content Planning
C.B. Cebulski, Editor-in-Chief

BLOOMSBURY ACADEMIC
Haaris Naqvi, Global Editorial Director
Leah Babb-Rosenfeld, Editorial Director
Hali Han, Assistant Editor
Ian Buck, Deputy Head of Production
Zeba Talkhani, Senior Production Editor
Ben Anslow, Senior Designer

First published in the United States of America 2026

Cover art: Mike Zeck and Terry Austin
Cover design: Ben Anslow

A catalog record for this book is available from the Library of Congress.

ISBN:	PB:	979-8-7651-4169-4
	ePDF:	979-8-7651-4168-7
	eBook:	979-8-7651-4170-0

Series: Marvel Age of Comics

Typeset by RefineCatch Limited, www.refinecatch.com
Printed and bound in the United States of America

For product safety related questions contact productsafety@bloomsbury.com.

To find out more visit www.bloomsbury.com/marvel-books

CONTENTS

"I did the best I could. I hoped it worked."

Jim Shooter

(*jimshooter.com, April 5, 2011*)

MARVEL®
SECRET WARS FAN MAIL
THE OFFICIAL MARVEL® NEWS MAGAZINE!
MARVEL AGE™
ONLY 35¢
20
NOV
LETTERS TO MARVEL SUPER HEROES™ SECRET WARS™
SECRET WARS
AR JIM: CAN'T WAIT FOR THE NEXT ISSUE TO FIND OUT IF
KEEP UP THE GOOD WORK!
DEAR JIM YOU'VE OUTDONE YOURSELF THIS TIME
DEAR JIM
DEAR JIM: WOW WHAT

1

Secret Wars Still Has Secrets to Tell!

Jim Shooter

"It's an idea that was created when Stan Lee started the Marvel Universe and had characters in a consistent universe and always running into each other and reading about each other in the papers and so on. Sooner or later it had to happen. So in essence I was fulfilling the destiny of the Marvel Universe."

(*Comics Interview* #14, 1984, interview by Jim Salicrup)

Destiny. Fate. Toy marketing. Sooner or later something like *Secret Wars* was going to happen. There were too many Marvel characters operating in the same areas, the same cities, the same worlds. Somebody was eventually going to bring them all together.

There had been crossover comics before where Marvel characters from one book would show up in another title. Marvel even published books like *Marvel Team-Up* and *Marvel Two-In-One* where Spider-Man and the Thing, respectively, would cross paths with various Marvel characters from Conan to Shang-Chi.

Stan Lee and Jack Kirby even brought back Bill Everett's 1939 creation Namor to guest-star in *Fantastic Four* #3 (1962). The Marvel DNA of crossovers and guest appearances and the scope of the Marvel Universe was there from the very beginning.

But nobody thought to bring everyone together for a twelve-part epic pitching an extraordinary cosmic battle between Marvel's heroes and villains.

Until Marvel's editor-in-chief met with Mattel, the toy company.

Comic books love origin stories, and that's the origin of the Marvel Alchemy that became *Secret Wars*.

Toys. Or, more precisely, toy companies.

Two toy giants were battling it out for their share of the market: Kenner and Mattel. That competition was going to change Marvel Comics, and Marvel Comics was then going to change the comic book industry.

The Mego Corporation had the toy license for both Marvel and DC. They declared bankruptcy in 1982 and closed in 1983.

The toy license for both comic book companies was now in play.

In 1976, Mattel CEO Ray Wagner had famously passed on the license to make *Star Wars* toys and action figures. That license eventually went to Kenner. Perhaps Wagner wasn't going to make the same mistake years later.

In the early 1980s, Kenner and Mattel were locked in a heated rivalry. Mattel had gotten the license for *He-Man and the Masters of the Universe* for action figures. After the collapse of Mego, Kenner signed a deal with DC Comics to license their super heroes for a toy line of action figures, vehicles, and play environments called *Super Powers*. There was a comic book tie-in series at DC that featured the work of Jack Kirby, one of the co-creators of the Marvel Universe.

Mattel needed to punch back to remain competitive. Wagner found that answer at Marvel Comics. According to Marvel's Editor-in-Chief Jim Shooter, Mattel's *He-Man* action figure line "was doing very well." Mattel "wanted to hedge their bet in case comic book character action figures became the rage."

That hedging involved creating a synergistic project between the two companies connecting toys and comics. Shooter said, "They came to Marvel to talk about licensing our characters. One thing they demanded of us was an 'event,' a special publication or series to help launch the toy line."

Shooter had some minor experience writing comics based

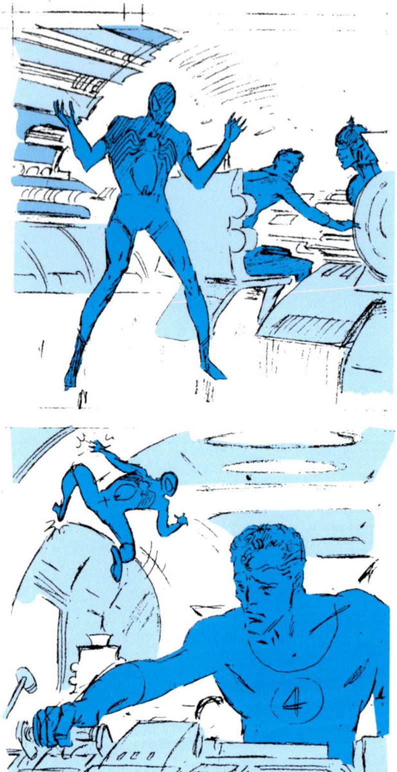

on a toy line. When he was 17 years old in 1968, he wrote the first two issues of *Captain Action* for DC Comics.

Thus, Shooter assigned himself as the writer.

Writing on his blog on April 4, 2011, Shooter explained: "When time came to actually do it, I realized that only I could write it. Marvel's writers at the time, some of the best in the business, were, to a person, very possessive about the characters they were writing. Allowing any one of the writers to handle pretty much everyone else's characters in *Secret Wars*, contemplated to be the biggest, most continuity-intensive crossover ever done, would have led to bloodshed in the hallowed halls. So, I wrote it."

And thus "Cosmic Champions" was announced in Marvel's own news magazine, *Marvel Age* #11.

Written in classic Marvel Bullpen Bulletins style, *Marvel Age* reported that: "We'll *tell* you where all of your favorite Marvel Super-Heroes disappear to so mysteriously at the end of the April cover-date books! They're off on an incredible adventure which joins all the major Marvel characters, pitting an all-star line up of heroes against a most frightful assemblage of villains!"

And then invoking the hyperbolic showmanship style of Stan Lee, this will be "an adventure which is so grand in scope that it takes a twelve-part special Limited Series to chronicle!"

The twelve-issue series would be published over a one-year period, but the events of the entire storyline would take place between the April 1984 cover-dated books and the May 1984 cover-dated books.

The *Marvel Age* article continued: "*Cosmic Champions* will do more than detail an awesome adventure—it'll explain the many *changes* that many of Marvel's heroes have undergone. Spider-Man gets a new costume! How the Fantastic Four lose a member—and gain a member! How the Incredible Hulk gets wounded! And how Kitty Pryde's pet dragon, Lockheed, falls in love!"

In *Amazing Heroes* #39 (cover dated January 15, 1984), an interview with Jim Shooter conducted by "J. Collier," a pseudonym of editor Kim Thompson, referred to the series as "The Secret War."

By the time the series debuted, though, it wasn't called

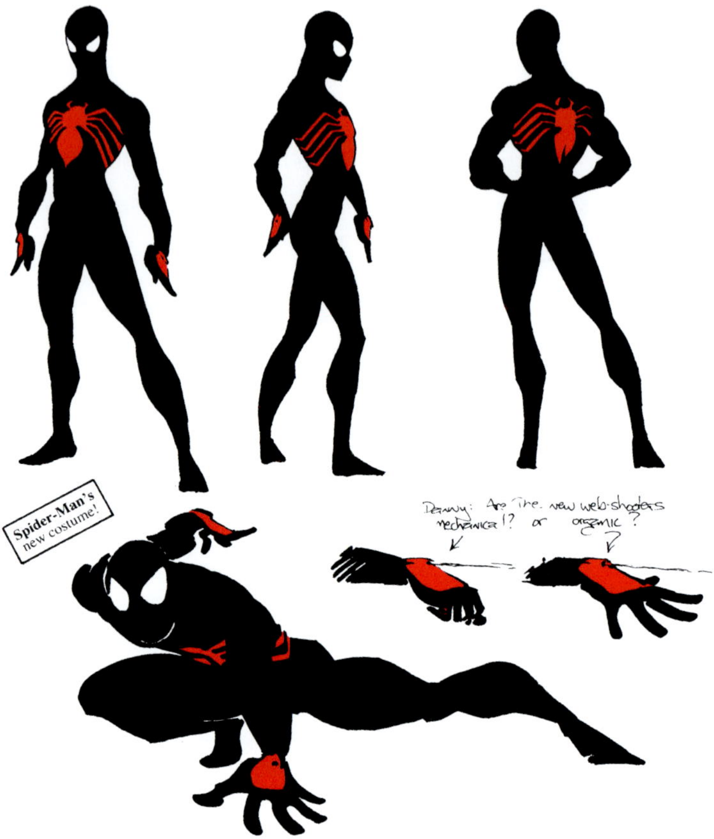

Cosmic Champions or even *The Secret War*. A full-page ad in *Marvel Age* #12 referred to the project as *Marvel Super-Heroes: Secret Wars.*

According to Shooter, "Mattel's focus group tests indicated that kids reacted positively to the words 'war' and 'secret.'" Without much of a struggle, the proposed series became *Secret Wars*.

The announced changes to Marvel's characters and storylines were just enough to plant the seeds that would cause many Marvel fans and retailers to get excited about the upcoming series and some to lose their minds over the promised changes. Many of those changes would appear in Marvel's regular titles before fans could see them happen in *Secret Wars.* That is some hard-core marketing guaranteed to pique fans' interest in checking out the upcoming issues of *Secret Wars.*

The new Spider-Man costume was a game-changer for Marvel fans. Some were vocal and negative about the change without realizing that big changes in comics are rarely permanent and often lead into unexpected directions. The new costume would be revealed as an alien symbiote and eventually evolve into a brand new character, Venom. If that's not Marvel Comics, nothing is.

The single page of original art by Mike Zeck and John Beatty from *Secret Wars* #8 that showed the first appearance of Spider-Man in his new costume would sell at auction in January 2022 for $3.36 million.

As Marvel's Editor-in-Chief and *Secret Wars* writer, Shooter selected the team that was currently enjoying a fan-favorite run on *Captain America*: penciler Mike Zeck and inker John Beatty.

Produced at breakneck speed, the twelve-issue *Secret Wars* mini-series had as much drama behind the scenes as on the page.

"The biggest problem with *Secret Wars* was that it was late from issue #1 to issue #12," Zeck explained. He added that Shooter was overseeing all of the other Marvel books at the same time. "It made for a less-than-perfect experience having to draw books just rush-rush-rush." Zeck said that a couple of times, including on the double-sized final issue, Marvel would rent a suite in New York City and fill it with other inkers, a letterer and colorist and "we'd have to stay up all night just to finish the last 5 or 6 pages."

Local New York-based inkers like Joe Rubinstein and Art Nichols would pinch hit because the deadlines were often too tight to ship last-minute pages from Marvel's New York offices down to Beatty in Florida. This was all pre-digital, when FedEx was king.

Despite the behind-the-scenes drama and the crush of what Marvel traditionally refers to as the "Dreaded Deadline Doom," all twelve issues came out on an acceptable schedule. They were wildly received by an audience eager to find out what would happen to their favorite heroes and villains, who would win and who would lose.

By killing off a major character during *Secret Wars* (and then reviving her with the help of an alien healer named Zsaji), and further creating a new costume for Spider-Man (a costume that was actually a symbiote), Marvel proved that anything could happen. Marvel also established a working template for epic event comics that continues to be followed today.

DC debuted their own super-hero epic, *Crisis On Infinite Earths* (cover dated April 1984), shortly after the launch of *Secret Wars*. DC’s event series had been in development for years and wasn't part of a toy launch. It was an effort to reset the company's complex continuity to streamline future storylines. DC famously killed off one of their own characters, Superman's cousin Supergirl.

Secret Wars was much more than a Marvel epic. It reset Marvel continuity to a certain degree, establishing a Shooter-based document for future stories. The toy line was only vaguely attached to the event that Mattel had demanded and it underperformed. The *Secret Wars* comic book, however, was a huge success, selling more copies than any comic book since the 1940s and launching an immediate sequel.

The following chapters will examine each issue in detail, punctuated with new reporting, interviews and anecdotes, and pointing out a few things that might not have been noticed the first time around.

So hang on, chums, pals, and true believers, there are secrets about *Secret Wars* you haven't heard yet …

Jim Shooter

"I offered an idea that was suggested by a dozen or so correspondents, usually younger ones, in the fan mail every day: one big, epic story with all (or many) of the heroes and villains in it. Everyone agreed."

(JimShooter.com, April 4, 2011)

Joe Russo

"Our love for Marvel is based on the books that we read as kids, the books that we fell in love with. The one series that we adored growing up was *Secret Wars*."

(Deadline, July 14, 2022)

Bob Layton

"It sounded impossible to me when I first heard about it."

(SyFy, March 4, 2019)

Jim Shooter

"I've really used the fact that all of the editors are here together. I have meetings all the time about it. They're dying to know what I intend to do and interested in keeping me posted on what they're doing so it'll work with their books."

(*Amazing Heroes* #39, January 15, 1984)

Danny Fingeroth

"I think we heard something about a Mattel deal. But Marvel did a lot of deals, so this one didn't stand out especially. At some point, I guess it was made clear to us that it wasn't just for an out-of-continuity comic that would be packaged with the toys, but for something else. I don't recall anyone in the office being especially interested or concerned about it."

Tom DeFalco

"We were not thrilled with the name."

(Syfy.com, March 4, 2019)

Ed Catto

"The whole 'Go big or go home' ethos was what *Secret Wars* was all about. They shook up the status quo—seemingly forever—and the fans loved it. And wanted more. So many of the Marvel and DC's big events since then have been about, to one extent or the other, trying to recapture that *Secret Wars* lightning in a bottle."

Paul Levitz

"Both DC and Marvel had gone out to license their toy rights because the Mego licenses faded away. We saw Mattel, Kenner, maybe one or two other players. We had serious bids from all of them and we ended up going with Kenner. And Mattel had been excited by what they'd seen so they said if we can't get DC let's get Marvel."

2

Avengers, X-Men, Fantastic Four, and More Assemble!

Before *Secret Wars* could begin, the characters had to get there from their own titles. Marvel Comics was a very New York-centric universe. The Marvel office was in New York. Staff and freelancers lived in and around the city. The comics used real New York locations whenever possible.

More importantly for Shooter's story, lots of Marvel's superheroes lived and worked in the area. That made it easy for Shooter to gather most of them together in Central Park—which is good, because the Beyonder's huge teleportation device arrived in the middle of it.

In *Amazing Spider-Man* #251, Peter Parker's Spider-Sense drew him to Central Park where "some sort of futuristic version

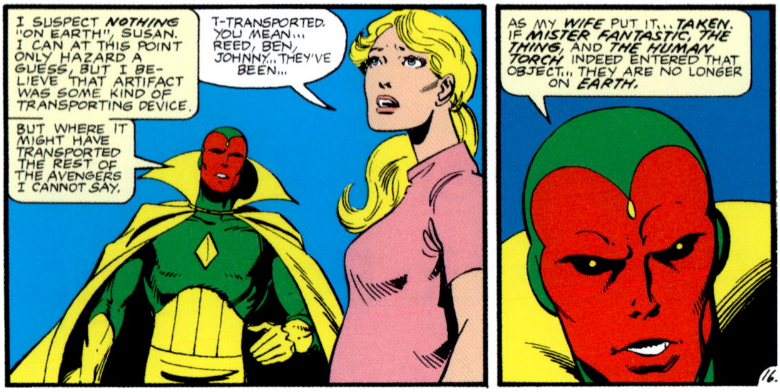

of Stonehenge" suddenly appeared. A powerful force pulls him inside and he disappears.

In *Uncanny X-Men* #180, Professor X pinpoints a "series of psychic scanning waves of incredible power." Within minutes, the X-Men walk inside the same device that Spider-Man did, and they disappear.

Then in *Iron Man* #181, Jim "Rhodey" Rhodes has been substituting as Iron Man temporarily while Tony Stark is in California. Rhodes is asked to investigate "some kind of strange energy emanating from Central Park." He disappears inside the same device.

The Hulk was cutting through Central Park in *Incredible Hulk* #294. He was on his way to rescue Dr. Katherine Waynesboro from Boomerang when the super-hero disappearing device caught his eye. Shortly thereafter, he vanishes.

In *The Thing* #10, Reed, Johnny Storm, and the Thing discover that the device has "a soothing effect, almost like a psionic tranquilizer." By the time Reed realizes it's a trap, they've already disappeared.

Over in *Thor* #341, the mighty thunder god arrives in New York to visit the Avengers. Moments later, Thor flies out with Captain America, Captain Marvel, She-Hulk, Wasp, and Hawkeye. They arrive in Central Park and disappear like all the others.

Avengers #242 expands on Thor's story. The Vision is picking up that same energy reading and because Central Park is "directly across the street" the whole group goes to investigate. Thor enters with a core group of the Avengers, and they disappear. The Vision believes they've been teleported elsewhere. Before the rest of the Avengers can act, the "entire mammoth structure begins to shimmer and fade, until it, too, is gone!"

At the same time in *Fantastic Four* #265, Sue Richards had noticed the bright light effect in Central Park. Even Alicia Masters saw it and she's blind. Sue loads up Alicia and Franklin into the Fantasticar, arriving in time to see the device and watch it disappear. She finds the remaining Avengers contemplating everyone's disappearance. The Vision suspects the machine was "some kind of transporting device," and that their friends, family, and co-workers are "no longer on Earth."

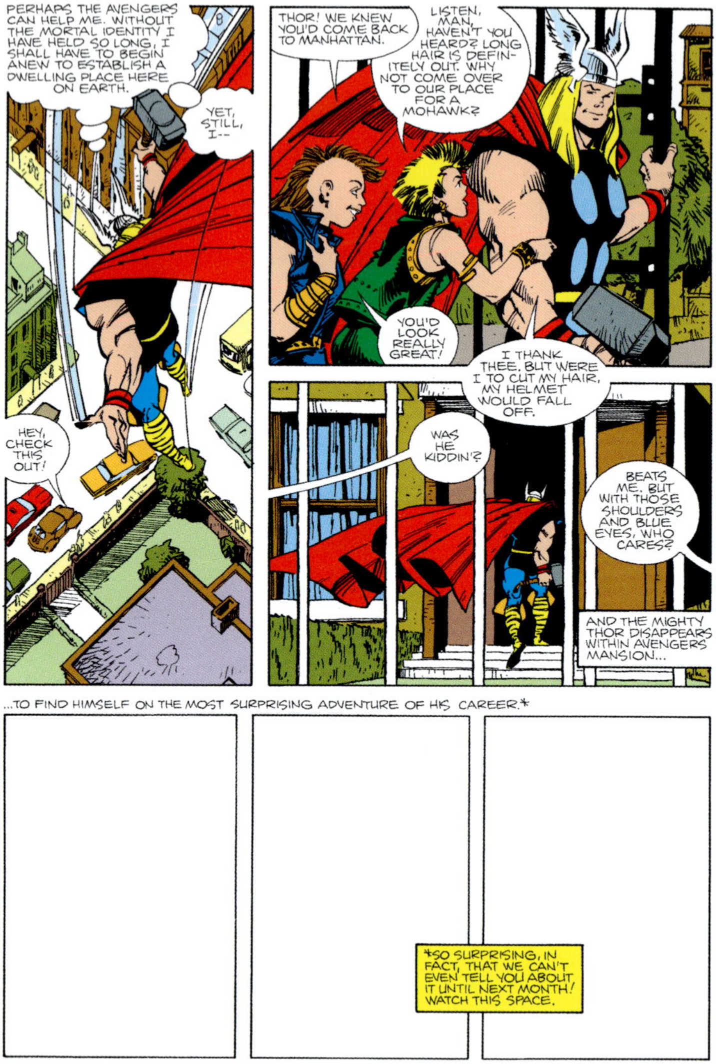

All of these issues end in cliffhangers and most of them have breathless captions urging curious readers to pick up *Marvel*

Super Heroes Secret Wars #1 to find out what happened. This is the first step of the genius of the marketing for the series.

The contest of champions had begun!

Peter Sanderson

"Editors and writers had to make adjustments in their own series to the fact that the characters were going off on this adventure in the midst of their regular continuity, and that some would come back changed, most notably Spider-Man in his black costume."

Steve Saffel

"*Secret Wars* was released shortly after the annual Toy Fair trade show in New York. It felt remarkable for there to be toys based on a comic book storyline, rather than a television show or animated series."

Paul Levitz

"Marvel didn't have a significant presence in Saturday morning animation. We had *Super Friends* that was still getting good ratings. Hanna-Barbera was prepared to remake it in whatever image was useful for Kenner and *Super Powers*. So I have to give Jim and his crew credit for coming up with *Secret Wars* and making it a comic book event."

Jim Shooter

"I guess I planned for the possibility of a sequel right from the beginning."

(*Amazing Heroes* #62, January 1, 1985)

3

Marvel Super Heroes Secret Wars #1

"The War Begins"
Writer: Jim Shooter
Penciler: Michael Zeck
Inkers: John Beatty
Letterer: Joe Rosen
Colorist: Christie Scheele
Editor: Tom DeFalco
Cover by Mike Zeck and John Beatty

Is everyone ready to rumble? The Marvel heroes have arrived aboard a floating space station far away from Earth. But questions remain—where, how, why, and to what purpose?

Reed Richards, aka Mr. Fantastic, uses his egghead powers to explain not only the how—teleportation—but the where:

#1 IN A TWELVE-ISSUE LIMITED SERIES
MARVEL®
© 1984 MARVEL COMICS GROUP
MARVEL SUPER HEROES™
SECRET WARS™
75¢
1
MAY
02475
APPROVED BY THE COMICS CODE AUTHORITY
CAN THE COMBINED MIGHT OF EARTH'S MOST POWERFUL SUPER HEROES DEFEAT THE ULTIMATE MENACE?!!

"It reassembled us inside a self-generated life-support environment."

It's a clever double-page spread with all the heroes. Mike Zeck and John Beatty do a really nice job with the body language of twenty and one dragon.

But there can't be a team without introductions. Shooter often said that any issue could be a reader's first one, so characters state their names and powers.

There's no time for team-building. They spot a second space station nearby. Xavier "mentally scans" that group which includes Galactus, Doctor Doom, Ultron, Enchantress, Doctor Octopus, Molecule Man, and several lesser-known villains like the Wrecker and his Wrecking Crew.

On his separate space station, Doctor Doom declares himself the most dangerous of them all. His "built-in sensors" have detected not only the other space station, but that it's filled with "those who think themselves heroes."

Shooter has a solid grasp on Doctor Doom's personality and captures the selfishness and power-hungry nature of one of Marvel's greatest villains. He also channels effectively the Shakespearean melodrama of Doctor Doom's dialogue as originally developed by Lee and Kirby.

This adds weight to everything that Doctor Doom says and it gives authority to his commands while making him seem even more confident. It gives an epic feel to the dialogue as it harkens back to his greatest adventures against the Fantastic Four.

Doctor Doom accurately puts his finger on the plot. It's "a gathering of forces … as if for war!"

Magneto, an ongoing nemesis of the X-Men and a self-described "master of magnetism," has been placed with the heroes instead of the villains. The Thing puts it succinctly: "What's this slime-ball Magneto doin' here?"

As ever, Magneto is just as pompous as Doctor Doom. "I find it more appropriate to ask why such as you were judged fit to be placed in *my* presence!" Sick burn.

There's no time for explanations, though, as both "constructs" travel through space to where "a planet is being formed."

It's so easy to show this in a movie or TV show. It's hard to do in comics, and Zeck and Beatty do an admirable job of highlighting the cosmic power that combines pieces from other worlds to create a patchwork fight-world.

In one panel, they draw a crowded star field packed with planets whose edges are being peeled away, revealing darkness. In the next, smaller panel, there's nothing but darkness as the galaxy is destroyed.

In the third, larger panel, pieces of different shaped-and-colored planets are crashed together to form the Battleworld. There's both energy and power in these three panels that run across the top of a two-page spread.

In a bit of absolute foreshadowing, Doom is clearly taken with the display. "The power necessary … it's incalculable, inconceivable!"

This is a super-hero comic book, after all, and villains in unfamiliar tight quarters will eventually have at it. Doctor Octopus and Absorbing Man are about to escalate, until Ultron goes full-on killer robot. Unable to process "the events transpiring," he declares: "I am Ultron! My purpose is to slay that which lives!"

Seizing a leadership role, Doctor Doom tries to enlist Molecule Man to stop Ultron, but there's a nifty twist. "I gave up being the Molecule Man!" says the villain who is "just plain Owen Reece now!"

What this change does is to mute Molecule Man's powers so that he's no threat to Doctor Doom or the others. It's a way to reserve his powers for later when they're really needed. It also gives a bit of humanity to the villains when Owen finds what could be true love.

Still, Doctor Doom urges Molecule Man to use his power to throw Ultron across the room. The mistake is that Ultron slams into the shins of the stiff-as-a-board Galactus.

Galactus uses his power to levitate Ultron so they are eye-to-eye. Then he "sucked the energy out through Ultron's mouth," snuffing him out "like a candle." Ultron collapses on the floor like a broken vacuum cleaner.

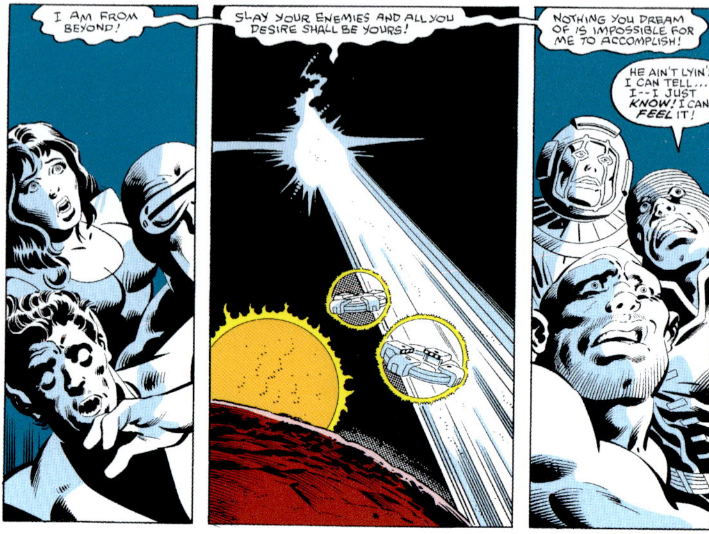

Out in space above Battleworld, a rift appears as if "opening in the void."

From that rift, the Beyonder speaks: "I am from Beyond!"

Not having the Beyonder reveal himself in some kind of licensable form might've seemed "cool" in 1984. In the modern era, however, that gimmick would never happen. A Beyonder action figure would now be a requirement of any licensing program. He would have to exist in physical comic book form so he could exist in plastic form with up to twenty points of articulation.

Though never seen, letterer Joe Rosen gives the Beyonder a creepy font that fits with his alien presence.

The Beyonder lays out his plan for the two groups that

he's brought together: "Slay your enemies and all you desire shall be yours. Nothing you dream of is impossible for me to accomplish."

Shooter had experimented with this idea in the past. In 1966, when he was 15 years old, he wrote "The Duel of the Super-Duo" for DC Comics (*World's Finest* #163). In that two-part story, Superman and Batman were lured to an alien planet to fight each other for the benefit of a villain named Jemphis.

Galactus responds immediately, and he's also the first character to call the Beyonder by name. The self-identified "devourer of worlds" senses the Beyonder can end his "ceaseless, monstrous craving for the very essence of living worlds!"

Galactus flies off toward the rift to confront the Beyonder.

Inspired, Doctor Doom follows in Galactus's wake, eager to discover "what secrets I might learn, what power could be mine!" Doctor Doom has started down a single-minded power-grabbing path that will see him through to the end of the series.

The Beyonder swats the planet-devourer like a fly. Doctor Doom is affected by the Beyonder's blast and both villains fall to the surface. Doom lets "my armor's computers try to analyze the alien forces which engulf me in hopes of gleaning some valuable shred of knowledge."

The Beyonder is moved to action. He sends the villains and heroes to different parts of his patchwork planet. On the

surface, Captain America immediately starts barking out orders. Reed stretches out, but reports there's "not a villain in sight."

Pointing to Magneto, Wasp disagrees. Magneto doesn't have an issue with it, deferring to the Beyonder for making the choice.

Xavier has no time for this type of distraction because the group needs to pick a leader. A group of Marvel heroes can't function without one.

After a lot of character back-and-forth, Xavier says that "no man in existence equals" the courage of Captain America. Thor backs that choice, saying that he will follow Cap "through the gates of Hades!" Case closed, and Cap is now in charge.

Meanwhile, far away …

Galactus is flat on his back, unconscious on the surface of

Battleworld. Doom finds "a fortress in the distance, provided no doubt by the Beyonder!"

In Doom's absence the group has been exploring the fortress's bounty of weapons. They've come up with a plan of their own: work together. They want Doom to lead them.

Doctor Doom, however, isn't interested in their "cheap lust." Doom suggests that they reach out to the Beyonder. "The key to totality, to immortality is near at hand, perhaps in our grasp!"

Doctor Doom feels the need to "seek out and take counsel with my most hated enemy." Conveniently, he finds a ship to take him where he needs to go. The ship is also easy to operate for "one of my intellect!"

Kang thinks Doom is off to join their foes. He finds a huge Kirby-style "gun" that is also easy to operate for "one such as I!" He shoots down Doom's ship with one blast.

This is classic storytelling by Shooter. In just a handful

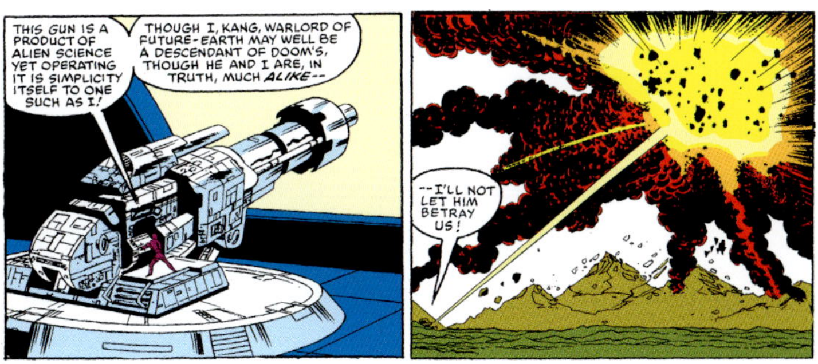

of panels, the heroes are established by putting aside their differences and finding a democratic way to work together. The villains, meanwhile, are instantly suspicious and paranoid, trying to assert dominance and looking only after themselves.

The heroes see the ship get blasted and rush to check it out, with Storm using her wind powers to carry any of the heroes who can't fly. Iron Man carries the rest on a large flat boulder, and it won't be the only time that funny visual appears.

What they discover is the wounded Doctor Doom, who miraculously survived.

Doom finally reveals that it's Reed Richards he must talk to, but senses "pity" from Captain America. Doom realizes he was a fool "to think such as you might comprehend what only Doom can know!"

Doom starts blasting the heroes and makes his escape, flying off-panel. Iron Man's radar picks up "bogies coming in fast!"

The "bogies" are a surprise attack from the villains. It's about to be: clobberin' time!

Star Trek reference

"… one minute we're checking out this giant whatchamacallit in Central Park, then—poof—the final frontier!"—Captain Marvel

The Marvel Age of Philosophy

"Extremism in defense of one's race is no evil."—Magneto

The Marvel Age of Trivia

Wasp is the first character to say "Secret War" (page 17, panel 5)

Wasp brings up events from *X-Men* #150 (October 1981)

When stretches the man

In nearly every panel he's in, Reed Richards is stretching, as if to just remind the audience of his only visual super-power.

Jim Shooter

"Some of it was dictated to us by Mattel. We had to have a headquarters so they could make a playset, and vehicles." (Syfy.com, March 4, 2019)

Jim Shooter

"Marvel's is a consistent universe where all the heroes know each other and have a cohesive background."
(*New York City Business*, February 11–22, 1985)

Mike Zeck

"I still saw no indication that Mattel was in any way involved with the direction of the comics."
(*Back Issue Magazine*, interview by John K. Kirk)

Dave Olbrich

"Marvel's original *Secret Wars* series came to the comic book industry like a kaiju in the mist. It was hard to see how big it would be or the power it would have. Once published, the size and scope came into view; fans, retailers, and Marvel's competitors braced for impact."

Steve Saffel

"Connecting the events of *Secret Wars* to the other titles seemed like the perfect opportunity to bring readers to characters they didn't already follow."

John Beatty

"(Jim Shooter) contacted Mike (Zeck) and my name was brought up as an inker. Mike called me to ink it and I accepted. I had been on *Captain America* for 2½ years. If someone is on a book that long, the establish a reputation for staying on a book and meeting deadlines. Mike and I were both ready for a change."

(*Comics Interview* #72, 1989, interview by Renée Witterstaetter)

Bob Wayne

"*Secret Wars* #1 was an enormous success for me as a retailer. I sold over a thousand copies at my store."

4

Marvel Super Heroes Secret Wars #2

"Prisoners Of War!"
Writer: Jim Shooter
Penciler: Mike Zeck
Inker: John Beatty
Letterer: Joe Rosen
Colorist: Christie Scheele
Editor: Tom DeFalco
Cover by Mike Zeck and John Beatty

Super-hero Fight Club has begun.

The heroes rally against an onslaught from the villains. Captain America embraces his new leadership role, telling everyone: "Avengers assemble! Form a wedge! I'll take the point!"

In addition to using their powers, the villains now have

MARVEL
2 IN A TWELVE-ISSUE LIMITED SERIES
MARVEL SUPER HEROES
SECRET WARS
© 1984 MARVEL COMICS GROUP
75¢
2
JUNE
02475
APPROVED BY THE COMICS CODE AUTHORITY

a *Star Wars*-style walking tripod driven by Piledriver and Bulldozer. It looks like a design for the *Secret Wars* toy line. The concussion weapons from the tripod prove formidable.

Kang laments the absent Doctor Doom and "how unfortunate that I had to slay him!"

But is Doom dead? Oh, hardly.

Doom is less than a dozen miles away, soaring through the alien atmosphere, courtesy of "his hidden jetpack." He lands where Galactus still lays immobile on the ground. Galactus stirs, rises from the ground and sets himself upright.

Doom sees this as an opportunity to communicate with the planet-eater. He calls out to Galactus, but is ignored "as if I was a gnat buzzing at his feet!"

Doom then makes a decision that will set in motion his actions for the rest of the series. Enthralled by the "all-powerful Beyonder," he does not want to "worship at the feet of this god-like being."

This is a strong sense of foreshadowing from Shooter, and one of his strengths. Despite the arrival of this new villain to the Marvel Universe, the story feels like it's going to twist back to center on the classic villainy of Doctor Doom.

Shooter has made story decisions that push Doom to act like Doom and be his authentic self. Drawn to the Beyonder's power, unable to make a deal, and only interested in his fellow villains as tools to be used, Doom is very on-brand.

This is an excellent story choice because the Beyonder is an invisible and unknown entity. Doom is known to both the heroes and the villains. They will be making choices based on what they know about Doom and by reacting to what he does. The story will become deeper and more personal, and not just a contest to please the Beyonder.

Secret Wars, then, is not going to be the Beyonder's story. It's going to be Doom's. Shooter's going to anchor the cosmic storyline around character.

Doom proceeds to "this fortress provided by the Beyonder" where he hopes to find something that will serve his needs. After destroying the fortress's defense drones, he discovers "the inert body of Ultron."

Back at the battlesite, the heroes are turning the tide. Cap, Thor, and Hulk are joined by an optic blast from Cyclops. She-Hulk faces off against the Enchantress, knocking out the Asgardian with a massive left hook.

With multiple villains fighting multiple heroes, Zeck and Beatty do a credible job of keeping the action clear and crisp. As the writer, Shooter is very good at establishing where everyone is and showing the consequences of every fight.

The Wrecking Crew and the unconscious Enchantress are captured. Cap sends Storm into the sky to look for "any defensible shelter around here!"

She finds a place provided by the Beyonder that, according to the Hulk, is "bigger than fifty-four and a half Pentagons!"

Inside, Reed secures the captured villains in a "prisoner-detention system we found." Conveniently, Reed also found a "healing device, a cell regenerator" where he's placed the Enchantress.

The cell regenerator becomes the "Chekhov's Gun" in the series. Introduced in this minor way, the regenerator is going to play a major part in wrapping up the series and defeating the Beyonder. So, spoiler alert.

Hours later, the remaining villains have gathered at their own fortress and encountered Doom. The villains are eager to finish what Kang started.

They are blasted from off-panel. Doom has rebuilt Ultron and armed him with "alien energies" from somewhere. He is now Doom's to command, and that puts Doom in charge of the villains.

Doctor Octopus correctly thinks that Doom's ambitions go

beyond the Beyonder's "little contest." He wonders if Doctor Doom will destroy the other villains while trying to achieve them or wait 'til afterwards.

Doctor Octopus and Doctor Doom are two of Marvel's greatest classic villains, both dating to the early 1960s. If anyone knows how Doom's mind works, it would be Doctor Octopus.

Doctor Octopus confines himself mostly to Spider-Man's world and Doom is more global and cosmic. Both are intelligent, narcissistic, criminal scientists. They have similar personalities, just different goals.

Regular Marvel readers know that Doom is never a team player. Shooter builds this up throughout these early issues with Doom working on his own plan and using the other villains only when he needs to.

That evening becomes a night of self-reflection. Wasp is "holding back a flood of despair." She-Hulk admits that, beneath her own bluster, it's all she can do "to hold it together."

Reed theorizes that the Beyonder has "fixed little things that seemed to be wrong, or missing!" That includes Xavier's wheelchair that he no longer needs and Spider-Man's perpetually-filled web-shooters.

Mostly the heroes are just sad. Cyclops feels cheated by leaving his wife right when he was "on the verge of real

happiness." The Thing overhears their discussion and is reminded that he "probably ain't ever gonna see Alicia again."

Spider-Man is worried that none of them will make it home. The Human Torch says the Fantastic Four have been to space a bunch of times, so "we'll get back, believe me!"

These late night self-doubt sessions are brought to an end by the web-slinger's Spidey-Sense that has zeroed in on their base's power plant. He heads toward the problem, while the Human

Torch heads off to round up reinforcements by burning a "4" into the night sky.

As Marvel fans already know, the burning "4" in the sky is the Fantastic Four equivalent of the Bat-Signal.

While all these late night sharing and caring conversations have been taking place, Magneto has been up to no good. Once inside the heroes' base, he has a plan that involves "the power core which energizes this entire installation!"

Magneto wraps up Spider-Man in metallic equipment. He buries the other heroes under a pile of metal equipment banks because "none may touch the person of Magneto!" The master of metal makes his escape, saying his business isn't finished but doesn't yet explain what that business might be.

While trying to chase after him, though, the Thing reverts to Ben Grimm, his human form. His desire to be human is a long-running thread in *Fantastic Four*, so it's a clever twist for Shooter to bring this storyline onto Battleworld at the worst possible time.

A massive storm approaches their base. Cap suggests that "we're going to have our hands full right here very soon!"

Nicknames

Dating back to the time of Stan Lee, Marvel writers have always given their characters lighthearted nicknames. In this issue, the Human Torch refers to Spider-Man as "Webs," and Spider-Man calls the Human Torch "matchstick." Storm refers to herself as a "mutant weather-witch."

Outdated sports reference

Iron Man answers a question from the Human Torch with "Does Doctor J play roundball, junior?" Julius Erving played professional basketball from 1971–1987.

Sports trivia

The Thing is revealed as a Mets fan, and laments that he can't watch one of their games on Battleworld.

Outdated teen slang

She-Hulk says "tubular, you know, to the max!"

Jim Shooter

"I think I included some of the toy stuff, but Mattel pulled some bait and switch. They showed us things that they later ended up using for He-Man and stuck the Marvel license with cast-off gadgets and items."

(JimShooter.com, April 5, 2011)

Mike Zeck

"The book was consistently pushing the deadline. In most cases I was working in a breakdown style to get the pages out, and if there wasn't time to get the pages to [John] Beatty, other inkers were called in to do backgrounds while John did foregrounds."

(*Comics Interview* #72, 1989, interview by Renée Witterstaetter)

5

Marvel Super Heroes Secret Wars #3

"Tempest Without, Crisis Within!"
Writer: Jim Shooter
Penciler: Mike Zeck
Inker: John Beatty
Letterer: Joe Rosen
Colorist: Christie Scheele
Editor: Tom DeFalco
Cover by Mike Zeck

A massive storm of "incomprehensible power" does indeed rage across Battleworld.

Safe in his lair, Magneto frees Wasp from his metallic prison that had he balled her up in during last issue's battle.

She sees Magneto fully chilled in what looks like a 1950s-era bachelor pad. Relaxing, he snacks on alien food and enjoys a

#3 IN A TWELVE-ISSUE LIMITED SERIES
MARVEL
MARVEL SUPER HEROES
SECRET WARS
THE CRISIS WITHIN!
75¢
3
JULY
02475
APPROVED BY THE COMICS CODE AUTHORITY
© 1984 MARVEL COMICS GROUP
ZECK

refreshing beverage. After he warns Wasp to not attack him, she uses her Wasp's Sting to upend his snacks.

Magneto says that since they are trapped by the weather he suggests a truce. Wasp tells Magneto, "It's your nickel," which sounds like something Ben Grimm might've said to Reed Richards in an early issue of the *Fantastic Four*.

Magneto's not much for snappy patter, and gets to the point that he's "not the monster you believe I am." Artists Zeck and Beatty really capture the casualness of Magneto's body language.

Meanwhile, hundreds of miles away, at the heroes' HQ, the storm still rages. A crackle of alien lightning strikes a massive rock that overhangs above. Ben and the Human Torch fear they're not long for this world.

From atop their HQ, the mighty Thor swings Mjolnir and hurls it at the falling rock. It's destroyed, and smaller boulders bounce harmlessly off the roof.

This is the first time that Thor's had some solo action in

the series and Zeck and Beatty make the most of it. As the rock splits, and the pieces scatter past Thor, he delights in his victory. Zeck and Beatty give him an expression of total satisfaction.

The storm has created a quiet time for the heroes inside, and they do some self-reflection. While She-Hulk carries around a giant piece of Kirby-style equipment called a "30-ton particle accelerator," Hawkeye confesses that he misses his new bride. Iron Man and Captain Marvel explore their facility for damage. In the "complex's vast central communications chamber," Hulk, Cap, and Reed discuss strategy. Hulk carries around "a modulator" that he will connect to She-Hulk's particle accelerator and that will "repair all the damage done by Magneto."

As a writer, Shooter understands the importance of downtime to pace a comic book between fight scenes and other action. Here he gives some quiet moments to the characters, but he also puts several of them to work making repairs. In addition to the character beats, it also gives Zeck some cool Kirby-adjacent equipment to draw.

While the storm rages, Reed uncharacteristically decides to

take a nap. A cycle of exhaustion and rest will be a recurring pattern throughout the series.

Stan Lee is famous for giving super heroes human flaws and relatable personal problems. Throughout *Secret Wars*, Shooter brings that classic Marvel element into the story to humanize both the heroes and villains. Here he lays out the toll that super combat can take on even the mightiest Marvel characters. It also gives the story a chance to slow down a bit while preparing for the next battle.

Meanwhile, Spider-Man has been swinging from the ceilings of their headquarters to help him feel at home. He stumbles across a meeting of the X-Men, who have kept themselves separate from the other heroes.

During his acclaimed run in the regular *X-Men* comics, writer Chris Claremont had positioned the team as a metaphor for marginalized groups. In *Secret Wars*, Shooter expands on that and has the X-Men wary of both the heroes and the villains. Unlike the villains on Battleworld, the X-Men don't express their concerns through violence.

In *Secret Wars*, the X-Men are united in remaining independent from the rest of the group. Led by Xavier, they're planning to find their own way off the planet. For that, "we go to join Magneto!"

Spider-Man doesn't like what he's heard and is going to "rat on you!" Spider-Man web-swings and dodges attacks from

Colossus, Wolverine, Rogue, Nightcrawler, and Storm, all while keeping up some character-driven banter.

Nightcrawler is impressed, calling Spider-Man "awesome." Cyclops tries to explain that what he overheard is "not what you think." Spider-Man escapes and seconds later runs into Reed.

Spider-Man tries to tell him, but his memory can't seem to recall it. Xavier used his "psionic abilities" to re-order Spider-Man's mind because so much is at stake.

Meanwhile, Xavier has conveniently discovered that one of the ships is easy to operate. Despite the still-raging storm, he wants everyone to fly to Magneto's fortress to pitch an alliance.

At Magneto's place, though, he's on a video call with Doctor Doom, telling him that "I am not interested in an alliance." That's enough for Doom to respond that if Magneto does "not serve me, I must consider you an enemy!"

Magneto returns to his "captive," Wasp. He senses she's warming to him, as if Stockholm Syndrome works that fast. He believes they may have reached "the beginnings of an understanding."

Just listen to Magneto's smooth line: "We agree that when my eyes meet yours that there is something electric!" Wasp isn't having any of that yet. "I don't remember agreeing to that!" she replies. Three panels later, however, they kiss.

By this time in the narrative, Shooter has set up a number of plot threads that will push the series forward. It's a delicate

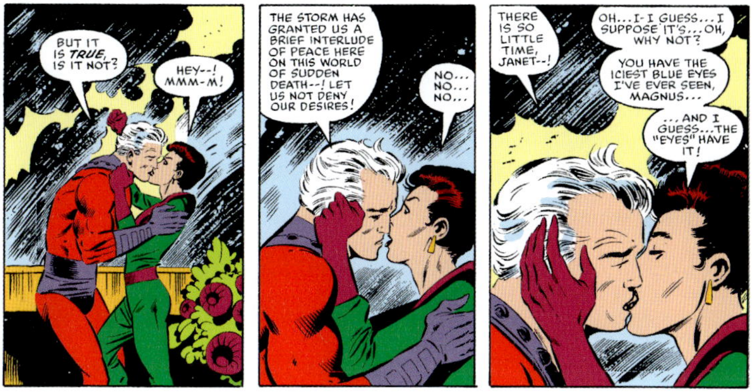

balance to cut through the various groupings and characters with enough plot to advance the story. He likely learned how to structure a multi-character story while writing "Legion of Super-Heroes" adventures for DC editor Mort Weisinger in the 1960s.

Doom is in a lab inside the self-named "Doombase." Rebuffed by Magneto, he's working with alien technology that is "so rich, so subtle … so easily harnessed to serve" his purpose. That purpose? He's making new super-villains.

When the Beyonder built Battleworld he combined pieces of other planets and mashed them together. One of the pieces came from Earth: a suburb of Denver, Colorado. In that suburb that's now on Battleworld, Doctor Doom has plucked two attractive women for his experiment.

Mary "Skeeter" MacPherran and Marsha Rosenberg are in clear chambers attached to undefined technology. Combined with the power of the planet's convenient storm, the technology converts the women into super-villains, Titania and Volcana. They emerge from their respective chambers with new powers and super-villain costumes. Doom holds out a spiked leather collar for one of the women, and that is clearly a choice. This raises questions, which go unanswered for now.

As a teenager, Shooter was a fan of Marvel Comics. When he started writing "Legion of Super-Heroes" stories for DC, one of the first things he did was try to incorporate Marvel-style storytelling into his work. That included creating new

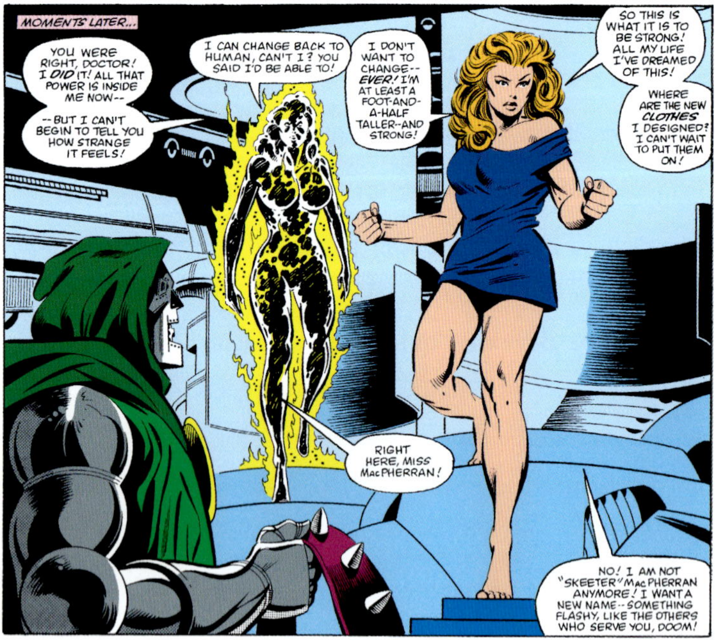

characters, especially super-villains. Twenty years later, he was still doing it.

New characters can provide a jolt to a story and shake things up. The reactions of existing characters to the newcomers can reveal other layers of personality. In this case, Titania and Volcana add female strength to the all-dude villains.

Titania is super-strong, while Volcana "is composed of ionized plasma—like the core of a star!" After a quick demonstration of each of their powers, Doom introduces them to the rest of the villains at Doombase. Once again, introductions are made for the benefit of the audience who may not have seen issues #1 and #2.

In classic Marvel fashion, Shooter doesn't get into the details of what happened to the planets after pieces were removed from each to form Battleworld. It becomes one of many dangling plot threads in the series that allows other writers to pick them up months or even years later.

Volcana thinks the massive storm on Battleworld is impressive. Molecule Man "could disperse the storm" because "I control molecules." His therapist has advised him to "let things take their natural course," however.

Heroes and villains in therapy may not have been an entirely new concept in 1984, but Shooter gets some good mileage from it. It sets Molecule Man's personality apart from the other villains. The reason for his therapy also ties back to Marvel continuity, so like any good Marvel writer he's using the past to inform the present.

Down in the lower levels of super-hero HQ, Thor opens the "special cell-regenerative healing capsule" that holds the unconscious body of the "beautiful Asgardian goddess" Enchantress.

Thor needs to talk to her about "things which only gods may speak." She opens up an enchanted portal and says they can talk, but elsewhere. Thor reminds her that she is still his prisoner. "Perhaps," she says coyly. This is a clever character-driven scene from Shooter. By using Enchantress's obvious charms, Shooter is able to get one of the mightiest Avengers away from the upcoming battle against the villains. That way the heroes can lose and Thor can play a role in their rescue.

Meanwhile, Hulk is having trouble concentrating: "The ideas, the answers used to come so easily." He's been thinking so hard that he let Cap oversleep. Now the sun is up and the storm has cleared. Cap orders Hulk to "sound the alarm" and get everyone "to battle stations."

Cap is correct, because a ship filled with villains rams into their HQ. By the time Reed, the Human Torch, and Ben Grimm realize they're under attack, Titania has already kicked in the door to their quarters. Reed and Ben are knocked unconscious. The Human Torch has broken ribs and a broken left arm. He blasts Titania, then quickly cuts a hole through the floor and disappears with his teammates.

She-Hulk is surprised by Volcana who blasts her, then drops heavy machinery on top of her. Captain Marvel, who appears to be enjoying a relaxing hot tub experience, is knocked unconscious by Doctor Octopus once she gets dressed. Hawkeye manages to scare him off with his "high tech arsenal of arrows."

Iron Man and Spider-Man are knocked down by Ultron, who can't see or sense either hero. Hulk tries to fight back by challenging Doom, but Molecule Man pushes him away with a giant rock.

Cap seeks to rally everyone to pull back and "retreat to a defensible position!" By the time the heroes have gone, Wrecker has returned with the freed villains, but "couldn't find Enchantress!"

The group had "fewer kills than" Doom had hoped, but feels they have "accomplished much here today." It's time to level the whole building.

The Marvel Age of Trivia

This issue features the first appearances of Titania and Volcana.

This is the first time in the series that Iron Man uses his new Jet Skates on his feet.

1970s insult

Hawkeye yells at Doctor Octopus to "Get away from her, turkey!"

Jim Shooter

"Wonderful, gentle, sweet [Marvel staffer] Mary Mac[Pherran] was indeed a smidgen of the basis for Titania, who was a willowy young woman who became uber-robust and Hulk-level strong. If MM minded that I had a tough bad-girl inspired by her, and made the nod in her direction, she never mentioned it. And wicked-smart Volcana had a bit of Mary Jo Duffy at her core. It was a thing we did back when."

(JimShooter.com, December 7, 2011)

6

Marvel Super Heroes Secret Wars #4

"Situation: Hopeless!"
Writer: Jim Shooter
Penciler: Bob Layton
Inker: John Beatty
Letterer: Joe Rosen
Colorist: Christie Scheele
Editor: Tom DeFalco
Cover by Bob Layton

This issue kicks off with the series' most iconic cover thus far. Bob Layton penciled and inked this homage to artist Jim Steranko's cover of *Incredible Hulk King-Size Special* #1 from 1968. Hulk holds up a massive piece of rock and earth, trying to prevent his compatriots from being crushed.

Bob Layton takes over the penciling chores in the first

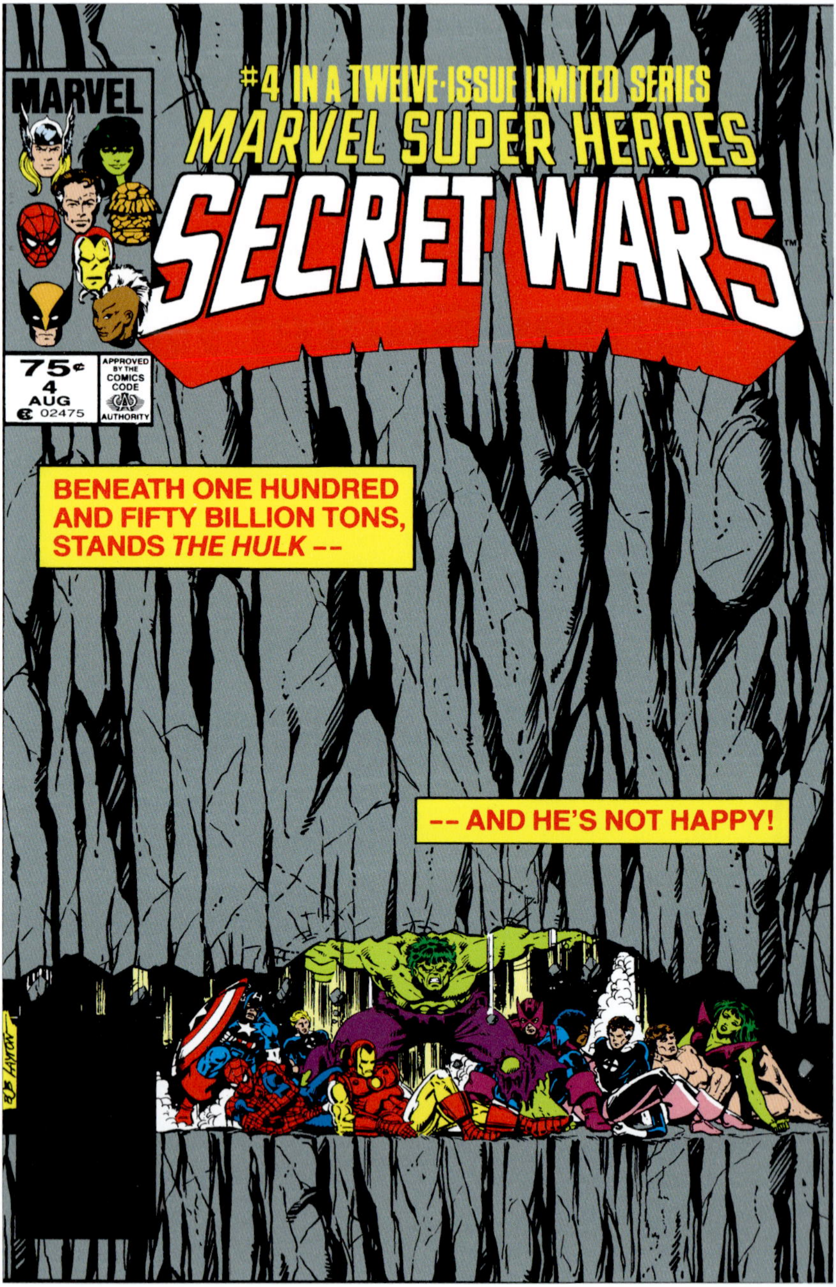

MARVEL
#4 IN A TWELVE-ISSUE LIMITED SERIES
MARVEL SUPER HEROES
SECRET WARS™
75¢
4
AUG
02475
APPROVED BY THE COMICS CODE AUTHORITY
BENEATH ONE HUNDRED AND FIFTY BILLION TONS, STANDS *THE HULK* --
-- AND HE'S NOT HAPPY!

of a two-issue fill-in. Inker Beatty described the production schedule and deadlines for *Secret Wars* as "brutal," so it's no surprise that a guest penciler shows up to help out Mike Zeck.

Layton draws characters that are longer and leaner, yet still in keeping with the style that Zeck has established in the series. Layton shows real skill when he has to fit multiple characters in a panel and he's very good at staging both the fight scenes and the quiet moments.

Following the surprise attack on the heroes' headquarters, the villains, led by Doom, destroy it. There's no sign of any of the heroes. Doom says "their moments are numbered" and "we shall hunt them down like dogs!"

Meanwhile, Volcana apparently can't resist the charms of Molecule Man. She gushes about the power he controls "with just a wave" of his hand. Flattered, he tells her to call him "Owen." A romantic connection enters its early stages.

Doctor Octopus locates the heroes about five miles away from the blast area. They're regrouping but in "bad shape! Easy to finish off!" Instead of using weapons, though, Titania proposes to do it herself. She lifts a huge piece of the wreckage and hurls it towards the heroes.

Molecule Man has a better idea. He uses his power to raise a mountain range into the air and floats it toward the unsuspecting heroes.

Cap regroups the heroes from the attack, but it's clear that

Reed, Spider-Man, She-Hulk, Ben Grimm, Captain Marvel, and the Human Torch are injured.

The X-Men are nowhere to be found, which causes some grumbling amongst the others. Hawkeye says the X-Men "apparently vanished before the battle."

There's no time for grumbling because the wreckage that Titania threw arrives. Fortunately, an uninjured Hawkeye splits it with one of his explosive arrows. Cap notices that Molecule Man's "mountain range which would dwarf the Andes looms above them." It falls on the heroes, seemingly crushing them like a giant shoe.

One hero is not accounted for, though.

Thor.

Since he released the Enchantress from her prison, the two of them have been chatting. Enchantress confesses her love for Thor, "because for millennia, I have desired you!" Thor does not know that he can return her love. Before they can kiss, however, they're interrupted by the crash of the mountain range on Thor's pals.

Thor and the Enchantress arrive in the middle of the group of villains who have been admiring their handiwork at squishing the heroes. Doom points out that all of Thor's team has been slain and that it's now thirteen against one. Thor hopes to enlist Enchantress to his side, but in a really nice two-panel

sequence by Layton and Beatty, Enchantress makes it clear that Thor is on his own. "So be it," Thor responds.

What follows is an epic fight as Thor takes on the Wrecking Crew, Titania, Kang, Doctor Octopus, and the rest. Before the villains get any traction, however, Thor disappears following a blast from Ultron. Surprise! Doom rebuilt Ultron and added "a disintegrator."

With Thor "disintegrated," Doom has Ultron slay Kang. Doom hasn't forgotten that Kang tried to kill him back in the first issue, and Doom never forgives. As the villains return to Doombase, they don't notice that the figure of Thor is watching them from safely behind a large boulder.

Magneto is still working his charms on Wasp. He pulls "metallic particles from the very air" and shapes them into a simple comb for Wasp's unruly hair. Wasp wishes Magneto had indoor plumbing, while he drinks a cup of "delicious alien fruit nectars."

There's no time for the duo to enjoy these simple pleasures because the X-Men arrive. Shooter continues the Marvel tradition of humorous nicknames as Wolverine refers to

Magneto as “Maggie.” Xavier proposes that Magneto and the X-Men join forces. Magneto was thinking along those very lines, based on what the Beyonder told them. Magneto doesn’t want to fight a defensive battle like Captain America. “We must slay Doctor Doom and his lackeys!”

Once Magneto wins and has the power the Beyonder promised, he will create “a golden age on Earth … in which men and mutants live together in peace!” He claims that Wasp agrees with him, and that’s a big mistake.

“You’re a great kisser, Magneto, but like a lot of men you presume that once you romance a woman her mind turns to mush and then you own her!” She makes her escape from Magneto’s lair to warn Cap.

Wasp has trouble figuring out the controls of her escape vehicle. It bobbles across Battleworld as she struggles towards the headquarters she thinks is still standing.

Deep under the planet’s surface, buried under tons of rock and earth, the heroes are still alive, breathing in a small pocket of air. Iron Man and Hulk “wedged out a space” as the mountain fell on them. Now Hulk holds up “two miles of rock,” giving them time to make a plan.

Using a larger panel to establish the dilemma the heroes are in, Layton switches to a series of taller, thinner panels that mirror the heroes being squeezed. It also creates an urgency to get them out from under the earth.

Reed immediately has a science-based plan. Like a stretchable MacGyver, he combines electronics from Iron Man's armor and "micro-electronic components" from Hawkeye's arrows with "circuitized relays" from Spider-Man's web-shooters.

This allows both Captain Marvel and the Human Torch to channel their powers through Iron Man. The super-charged hero aims his turboed repulsors towards the surface, tracing a slight tapping sound from above.

KTHOOOM!

Freed from underground, the heroes discover the tapping from the surface was Thor using Mjolnir to try to locate them. But how did Thor escape the villains? He "used a flash of lightning to blind" the villains while he escaped.

Cap sends Captain Marvel to go shopping for food, shelter, and medical supplies. What she finds is an alien village in the shadow of Galactus. The villagers don't mind Galactus looming large, but they seem fearful of the heroes. Letterer Joe Rosen does an excellent job of capturing the alien speech with a series of swoops and swirls that almost resemble cursive.

One young woman, identified as a "healer," puts her helping hands on the unconscious She-Hulk to show her powers. It's on Johnny Storm that she really shines, as he notes "my ribs and arm feel better already!" Naturally, Johnny hits on her, because she's the first single woman he's seen in four issues.

While the alien healer never touches human Ben Grimm, he inexplicably changes back into the Thing. Reed is spared contemplation when he notices that Galactus has moved his arms upward towards the sky. Reed is horrified, and that's a great cliffhanger for this issue.

Number of Hitler references in this issue: two

Wasp (to Magneto): "And now that I know you really, really are the most evil scum since Hitler—I'm going to stop you!"

Professor X: "In that moment of weakness, I was no better than Doom … or Hitler … or anyone else who ever used power to usurp another's freedom."

Oddball 1980s music reference

"I'll Tumble 4 Ya" (1983) by Culture Club, featuring Boy George.

Bob Layton

"When Mike started running into deadline problems, mainly from the sheer complexity of the series, I was asked to jump

in and buy him some time since I had no regular monthly assignment at that moment. I was simply filling in for a very tired friend of mine."
(SyFy.com, March 4, 2019)

Pat Brosseau

"At Marvel Joe Rosen was always the favorite letterer of all the letterers. His never too flashy, smaller than usual lettering and thick balloon shapes made his lettering instantly recognizable and loved by many an editor there. His wonderful sound effects worked to serve the art and never overpower it. His alien lettering for *Secret Wars*, with its cursive-like beauty, showcased the consummate pro's ability to make the lettering look elegant and alien at the same time."

Jim Shooter

"At the beginning, I was writing plots and Mike (Zeck) was drawing from them. I think that eventually we sort of segued into me doing the layouts. I kept finding in the plots it was easier to do the sketches of what I wanted than it was to spend pages explaining."
(*Comics Interview* #14, 1984, interview by Jim Salicrup)

7

Marvel Super Heroes Secret Wars #5

"The Battle Of Four Armies!"
Writer: Jim Shooter
Penciler: Bob Layton
Inker: John Beatty
Letterer: Joe Rosen
Colorist: Christie Scheele
Editor: Tom DeFalco
Cover by Bob Layton and Bob Wiacek

This is a "drug issue" that feels like it takes place at a yoga retreat in the Arizona desert. Bob Layton is back for his second consecutive pinch-hit issue. It's just in time to show off Galactus's massive ship that Iron Man says "takes up the whole sky!"

The aliens are afraid of what's happening. Johnny can't

MARVEL
#5 IN A TWELVE-ISSUE LIMITED SERIES
MARVEL SUPER HEROES
SECRET WARS
© 1984 MARVEL COMICS GROUP
75¢
5
SEPT
02475
APPROVED BY THE COMICS CODE AUTHORITY
AT LAST!
THE X-MEN STRIKE BACK!

get any answers out of his favorite "pretty lady" healer because he doesn't "dig her lingo." She seems to sense what Johnny needs and leads him by the hand into her home. Naturally, Johnny thinks they're going to have a little "R and R."

Instead, she has what looks like an alien hookah. The emitted vapors are "sweet but strong," and Johnny inhales deeply. Soon, he can feel his "mind is opening up like a book!" This is a pretty good exposition trick because it allows Shooter to bring readers up to speed from the previous issues.

Longtime Marvelites of a certain age might remember that Marvel had drug references in *Amazing Spider-Man* #96–98

in 1971. Those issues went to press without the Comics Code Authority's seal of approval.

By 1984, the code had been amended, and Johnny is in an alien woman's home inhaling hallucinatory smoke from an ornate vase on the floor. Marvel progress marches on.

The vapors lay out the story so far and Johnny understands so much of what's been happening. The vapors even helped Johnny discover the healer's name: Zsaji. And, of course, they kiss, as she learns to pronounce his name: "Jah-nee."

Back at Magneto's lair, shirtless Colossus "wallows in an ocean of loneliness and worry," with one thing on his mind: his beloved Kitty Pryde. He dreams of kissing her and building a life together once she's "old enough." But now those plans might never happen if the Beyonder doesn't send him back to Earth.

Colossus's fantasy-future is interrupted as the X-Men are called to meet with Magneto. The master of magnetism retracts the dome to his fortress and reveals Galactus's ship.

Magneto barks out orders to the X-Men. That rankles Storm, who's the supposed leader of the team, and Wolverine, who doesn't like taking orders. Cyclops somehow thinks he should be the leader because the stakes are so high.

Back at Doombase, Doom is ready to put his own plans into motion and orders his "Servitors of Doom" to be on red alert, ready to strike "at a moment's notice." Someone who doesn't listen to Doom is the Enchantress.

Even though she's "a goddess, beautiful, powerful, immortal," some barrier "prevents me from simply fleeing this world." She's eager to join forces with Doom so the two of them can escape together.

In return, she promises Doom "the love of a goddess for the rest of your life!" She even offers to heal the scars underneath his metallic mask. Doom doesn't take the bait, though. He knows she's acting and dismisses her.

"Very well, madman!" she threatens as she disappears in a puff of smoke. "'Tis done!"

Xavier has trouble accessing Galactus's thoughts, even with Magneto's assistance. The Human Torch thinks he has it figured out, though: "He's going to eat this planet right out from under us!" Reed isn't certain, but he would also like to talk to Galactus. He once saved Galactus's life back in *Fantastic Four* #244 so he figures, "I alone have a chance of communicating with him." Reed stretches all the way up to Galactus, calling his name like he's seen an old friend on the street.

Galactus doesn't answer Reed. Magneto and Xavier increase their psychic attack on Galactus, with Magneto turning it up to eleven. This causes a surge of "psionic feedback" that engulfs Magneto and Xavier. It also drops rubbery Reed back to the surface. The multi-panel flailing of Reed's extended body is very well done by Layton. It's an effective representation of how Reed's stretch powers work, and how he turns into a limp rubber band when things go wrong. Galactus raises his arms in the air and from his massive ship leaps a huge metallic warrior giving off Ultron vibes.

Galactus's robot has a few enhancements, especially hot goop that paralyzes the heroes, including Thor, Iron Man, and Hawkeye.

Still, Cap and the Thing work together so the Human Torch can melt the robot's insides, leaving it a smoldering husk on the ground. Destroying a larger villain by burning him from the inside out is a clever use of the Human Torch's powers and it's nice to see him get in on the action. But there's no time to relish the moment. Spider-Man's Spider-Sense kicks into high gear.

Just in time, as "Doom's men" arrive.

No matter what happens throughout the series, Doom says he expected it, was ready for it, and it fits in perfectly with his as-yet-unstated plans. There's no exception here as Doom uses the fight to distract Galactus because "a split second is all I need!" So he's up to something.

The battle between the heroes and villains looks to be going the way of "Doom's men." Huddled into a small group, awaiting a final assault, Cap tells the heroes to "keep fighting! We're not done yet!"

The caption "Suddenly" does a lot of heavy lifting as the X-Men arrive. As Magneto and Xavier stand by the sidelines, Xavier yells orders to his team to "press them hard!" The battle intensifies in just a few panels.

Layton excels in this epic battle scene. He mixes tight panels with expansive multi-character panels, creating a strong sense of movement and action. All of the characters are involved and it feels like a real battle is taking place.

Even in the middle of the fight, though, Colossus is motivated by thoughts of his young girlfriend. As he lifts Piledriver into the air with one hand and grabs one of Doctor Octopus's tentacles in the other he yells out, "I will smash all of you! You are what keeps me from Katya!"

Storm calls up the power of the planet's weather. Her storm is enough to distract Galactus's attention for just a moment. Doom seizes his chance and heads 22 million miles "at Tachyon speed" towards Galactus's massive ship. Colossus is eventually overwhelmed and wounded, causing an angry Cyclops to wide-blast the villains.

The "battered servants of Doom" are rescued by the Enchantress, who whisks them away to safety. At the same time, and much to the dismay of the X-Men, Xavier orders them back to their ship, leaving Colossus behind. Xavier theorizes that Colossus is too injured to be moved and best left in the hands of the village healer, Zsaji.

Xavier has a new strategy for the team. The X-Men will remain as independent allies of "Captain America's group." He wants them to be a "third force" and to assist when needed.

Colossus initially refuses to be treated by the healer, but after

Iron Man refers to her as "not a bad package," Colossus starts seeing her differently. Colossus lets Zsaji apply her healing hands. Instantly he feels better, and already jealous of the attention she pays the Human Torch.

So where's Doom? He made it inside Galactus's massive ship and wanders around exploring. Recognizing that he is but a virus inside a toy, he's determined to grow, "to become strong, to overwhelm this mighty, pulsing world-ship!" Once that's done, he plans to take out Galactus himself, and then the Beyonder. And he may have found something interesting in the cliffhanger of the last panel.

Molecule Man and his humblebrags

"I gained absolute mastery of all molecules!" (page 8, panel 1)

"I control all molecules!" (page 9, panel 2)

Outdated Coneheads reference

"Good thing they ain't never heard of rasslin' on planet Remulac!"

Cameo appearance by Flash Gordon reference

Iron Man refers to Zsaji as "this broad from Planet Mongo."

Jim Shooter

"Tom DeFalco's the editor. I pitch my plots to him and he always has a lot of good suggestions and gives me a lot of help on plots, and then after the pencils come back, after I write the story from my own layouts, Tom edits the script. Tom is extremely important and does a lot of work on it." (*Comics Interview* #14, 1984, interview by Jim Salicrup)

8

Marvel Super Heroes Secret Wars #6

"A Little Death …"
Writer: Jim Shooter
Penciler: Mike Zeck
Inker: John Beatty
Letterer: Joe Rosen
Colorist: Christie Scheele
Editor: Tom DeFalco
Cover by Bob Layton

An issue of big returns. After a two-issue breather, Mike Zeck is back as the series penciler.

Zeck seems to have benefited from the break. His art in this issue is more dynamic, the fight scenes are well-staged, and there are a number of panels that truly shine under John Beatty's inks and Christie Scheele's colors.

#6 IN A TWELVE-ISSUE LIMITED SERIES
MARVEL
MARVEL SUPER HEROES™
SECRET WARS™
© 1984 MARVEL COMICS GROUP
75¢
6
OCT
02475
APPROVED BY THE COMICS CODE AUTHORITY
BOB LAYTON

Also returning this issue is Wasp. She was absent all of last issue and missed the big battle. Where has she been? She escaped from Magneto's lair "in a stolen landskimmer." Wasp has difficulty controlling the ship and crashes on Battleworld's surface, all while blaming Galactus and the X-Men for setting her up to fail.

She takes out her anger on the "crazy car" and blasts it. She flies solo across the landscape. She finds a place to rest and also finds the Lizard.

Meanwhile, "several million miles from the surface of the patchwork planet," Doom fiddles with an "alien control console" within Galactus's ship. As with everything else on Battleworld, the controls are very intuitive. It isn't long before Doom has reconstituted the "strange vibratory energy" that his sensors picked up.

That reconstituted energy reforms as the old-school Marvel villain Klaw. This is a new incarnation of the classic Marvel villain. The new Klaw is goofy and weird, speaking in repetitive phrases and riddles. Doom has "managed to recreate a raving lunatic!"

Klaw gets several panels of exposition, recounting how he was converted to energy. Short version: The original Klaw was killed by Dazzler. Since he's made of "solidified sound," she absorbed all of his "sound-substance—just ate me all up!" When Galactus took Dazzler as his new herald, "she tried to fight him" and used Klaw's energy form as her "big energy burst." The leftover energy blip that once was Klaw oozed its essence into the framework of Galactus's ship. That's where he remained until Doom just now freed him.

With 30 days between regular monthly issues, some kind of recap is generally worked into each current issue. Throughout the series, Shooter uses a number of storytelling techniques to bring new readers up to speed and remind everyone what's happened so far. Shooter mixes it up with flashbacks, dramatic captions, a character's soliloquy, characters talking to a new character, exposition during an opening fight scene, or even a bold statement from a villain. Here Shooter brings in an existing Marvel character in a new form, as he pulls on the threads of Marvel's universe-spanning continuity.

Doom senses he might now be saddled with an idiot, and weighs his options.

He's going to have to distract Galactus using indirect means. If Galactus wants to eat the patchwork Battleworld, then perhaps "I can spoil his lunch!" Doom isn't really known for his dad jokes, but there it is. Doom beams Klaw down to Battleworld's surface with a message for his team of villains.

This means that not only has Doom figured out Galactus's equipment, he discovered some kind of Star Trek-like transporter and was able to use it without any trouble. Klaw's appearance surprises the villains at Doombase. Before he can give the group Doom's orders, the villains become divisive and combative. Titania refuses to take any orders from an idiot, and wants to rip Klaw in half. A furious Ultron recognizes that Klaw has given the proper code words from Doom and "the orders are genuine! They will be obeyed!"

Meanwhile, Wasp has made a new friend: the Lizard. He's been in the swamp for the last couple of issues. He's injured and she talks to him like he's a puppy she found abandoned by the freeway.

At Magneto's fortress, the X-Men recover from Galactus's psionic feedback. Fortunately, Magneto "shielded everyone inside bubbles of magnetic force," so they'll be okay. As the team starts making repairs, Xavier finds a comfortable chair. Even though on Battleworld he no longer needs his wheelchair, his legs "are not yet quite strong enough."

While psychically spying on the villains, Xavier learns Doom's plan to dispatch a task force of the villains "to a volcanic plane on the other side of the planet." Xavier appoints

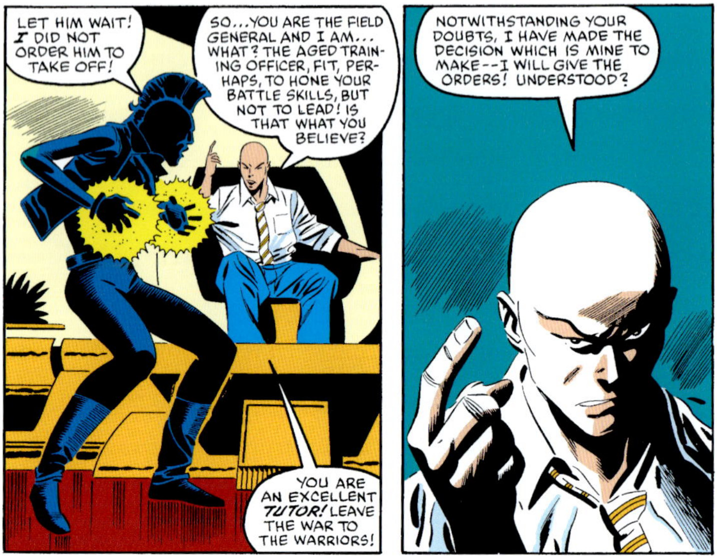

Cyclops to lead Rogue and Wolverine to investigate "and stop them if you deem it necessary."

Storm confronts Xavier, telling him that she's the rightful leader of the X-Men, "not Cyclops, not you!" She urges Xavier to "leave the war to the warriors!" In a very ominous panel by Zeck and Beatty, with some heavy lifting by colorist Scheele, Xavier has the final words: "I will give the orders! Understood?"

At the alien village, Colossus rests and recovers. As Captain America and his team help with repairs, Colossus wonders why these heroes have such a distrust of mutants and why they can't get along. Colossus would like to go back to his own team, and he would also like to go back to Earth to see his beloved Kitty Pryde.

Increasingly Colossus's thoughts turn to the alien healer Zsaji, who lays her hands on his chest and uses her energy to help his recovery. Four panels after declaring his love for Kitty, he now declares Zsaji is the "most beautiful, wonderful woman I have ever met!"

Cap rallies his team with a plan, in one of the best-drawn panels in the entire series. Using a stick to diagram his plan in the dirt, he lays out what they should do: "remain on constant alert." Galactus could start eating Battleworld at any moment.

She-Hulk is ready to track down Magneto and punish him for kidnapping the still-missing Wasp. The Hulk wants to go on the offensive and "smash Doom! Or even Galactus!" It's all Cap can do to hold this coalition of eager heroes together.

Slightly off to the side of the group, Hawkeye and Spider-Man share a moment. Since Reed poached Hawkeye's hi-tech arrows to enhance Iron Man's armor, he has to make more. Without arrows, Hawkeye's "just a guy in a funny suit." It does seem funny to see Hawkeye whittling new arrows out of local wood.

This is a strong insight into heroes that are just in great physical shape but don't have any super-powers. Shooter positions Hawkeye as very much aware of his position in the hierarchy and how important his tools are when fighting bad guys.

Iron Man, meanwhile, tries to make some time with Captain Marvel with a short "What's happenin', babe?" But she isn't having it. She takes off for the sky, wondering how she ever thought Iron Man was so "sophisticated, worldly." Maybe there's "a different man inside that armor."

Half a Battleworld away, though, Doom's team lands where Klaw instructed. Before they can get started on their mission, Xavier's trio of X-Men shows up. Cyclops correctly notes that if the villains are here, they're up to something and "we must prevent them from doing it!" Wolverine agrees: "Do or die! My kind of fight!"

Wolverine leaps at them, claws extended. Titania hurls a giant boulder and knocks Wolverine out of the air. Rogue says, "We don't stand a chance!"

Cyclops finally opens his "ruby quartz visor" and blasts the villains, putting them "back on their heels for a second." Molecule Man's powers shield the villains from the blast, but he still has time to request that they call him "Owen, or even Mr. Reece."

Rogue swings "around to hit them from behind." Her sneak attack doesn't work because Titania smacks her with a powerhouse left.

The battle rages until Wolverine gets the drop on Molecule Man. Before he can fully slice Owen into shreds, Cyclops deflects Wolverine with an optical blast. This allows Titania to backhand Wolverine almost out of the panel. Doctor Octopus picks up the injured Molecule Man. "He's hurt badly! Very badly!" They can't lose Molecule Man since he's important to Doctor Doom's plan. They retreat.

Cyclops explains to Wolverine that he had to stop him from killing Molecule Man because "if you want to be on our side, you don't kill!"

Rogue wants to know what the villains were up to, and Cyclops figures it has to be the "volcanic cones" that dot the landscape. With a "well-placed full-power shot" Cyclops blasts one of the volcanos. That triggers a chain reaction. The heroes barely make it out as the other volcanos erupt.

At the swamp, Wasp has finished dressing the Lizard's wounds. She thinks he's "been a very good patient" who might

"be a sweetie" underneath. The Lizard responds with "I hate humansss, crush them all!" As Wasp responds, a blast from off-panel hits her chest.

The reveal is Doctor Doom's team riding in a massive vehicle. Doom's orders are to bring in the Lizard because they "need his muscle for the big showdown!" The Lizard puts up a fight, but only for a panel because a "stasis-ray" from the rig grabs not only the Lizard but also Wasp's corpse. They'll "dump her on the way back to Doombase!"

At the local village, Galactus has nearly finished building his device on the mountaintop. The heroes want to do something to stall his progress. Cap says that Reed wants to make another attempt at reasoning with the planet-eater, "maybe at dawn." While they wait, though, a mysterious shadowy figure lurks in the foreground to tease the next issue.

The Marvel Age of Trivia

Verily doth Thor have but one line of dialogue in this issue.

Social tips from Iron Man

He refers to Captain Marvel as both "babe" and "that squeeze."

Outdated pop culture reference

The Human Torch sings the lyrics to Michael Jackson's "Thriller."

Personal grooming thoughts from the Wasp

"Oh no I broke a nail."

"Send my limo around! I want to freshen up, I want Vidal to do my hair, I want lunch at 21, and then I want a nap!"

"You'd better apologize or I'll tell Gucci where to find you!"

Marvel at the movies

An earlier incarnation of Klaw made two live-action appearances in the MCU, played by Andy Serkis:

Avengers: Age of Ultron (2015)

Black Panther (2018)

Jim Shooter

"Christie Scheele has earned a place up there with Glynis [Wein] and Marie [Severin]. Her colors bring *Secret Wars* to life, and no one's palette could have been more breathtaking." (*Marvel Age* #20, November 1984)

Jim Shooter

"Tom DeFalco, who edits the book, hates the limelight. Tom prefers to stay behind the scenes letting the work speak for itself … this guy does a phenomenal job day in and day out." (*Marvel Age* #20, November 1984)

Mike Zeck

"I had to tailor my art to what Shooter was looking for. *Secret Wars* was his baby and he had his own rigid view of what he wanted. That took away a little of my own creative input." (*Comics Interview* #72, 1989, interview by Renée Witterstaetter)

9

Marvel Super Heroes Secret Wars #7

"Berserker!"
Writer: Jim Shooter
Penciler: Mike Zeck
Inker: John Beatty
Letterer: Joe Rosen
Colorist: Christie Scheele
Editor: Tom DeFalco
Cover by Bob Layton

A new hero arrives while an old favorite dies! On the outskirts of the alien village, which doesn't appear to have a name, the shadowy figure from last issue's cliffhanger "steps out of the shadows into the light." It's Spider-Woman. Naturally, there are questions because she is "a different lady than the Spider-Woman we knew," says Cap.

#7 IN A TWELVE-ISSUE LIMITED SERIES
MARVEL®
MARVEL SUPER HEROES™
SECRET WARS™
© 1984 MARVEL COMICS GROUP
75¢
7
NOV
02475
APPROVED BY THE COMICS CODE AUTHORITY
THE DEATH OF AN AVENGER! THE X-MEN'S GREATEST BATTLE! AND, INTRODUCING THE ALL-NEW
SPIDER-WOMAN!

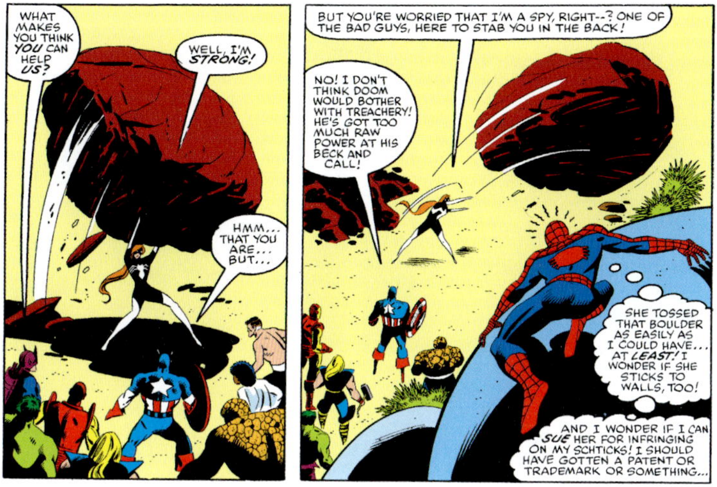

She was in a suburb of Denver when the Beyonder was patchworking Battleworld together from bits of different planets. She was scooped up and now she wants to join up. As proof of her skills, she tosses a huge boulder. Spider-Man wonders "if she sticks to walls, too" and if he "can sue her for infringing on my schticks!"

There's no time for discussion, though, because the villains in their big rig plow through the village, blasting in multiple directions. While the heroes scurry the villagers to safety, the Wrecker tosses Wasp's body to the ground and the rig races off.

Zsaji makes a valiant attempt at healing, but Wasp is dead. Most of the heroes want revenge. Cap says if they're all out avenging, then Galactus could start up his "world eating machine." If he does that, there's no stopping him and

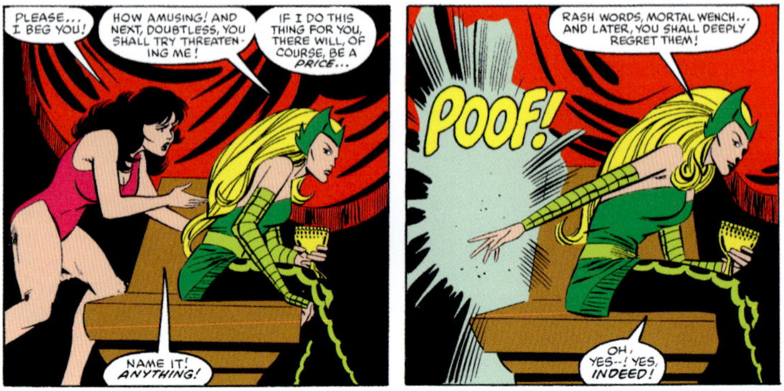

Battleworld would perish, "including these innocent villagers and all those people from that suburb of Denver."

Meanwhile, Rogue, Cyclops, and Wolverine rocket their way through the volcanic eruptions Cyclops triggered last issue. Xavier tells them to change directions to "pursue Doom's task force." Storm, Nightcrawler, Xavier, and Magneto board a convenient second skycraft to join them.

Back at Doombase, Volcana watches her wounded boyfriend on a monitor. She reaches out to Enchantress, asking her to use her magic to "transport me to my Owen!" Enchantress refuses to do it without exacting a price from Volcana. She agrees, and "poof!" Volcana is whisked away to her Owen.

The heroes' two skycrafts arrive to intercept Doctor Doom's crew and crash them to the surface. The villains pour out, ready for a fight.

Cyclops's optic blasts ricochet off Titania and send Rogue

flying. The Absorbing Man chases off Magneto. Xavier "cannot pierce our enemies' minds" because they are sealed. The noise of the attack is overwhelming his powers. Also, he's still wearing dress slacks and a white dress shirt.

The Absorbing Man absorbs "the property of these here rocks." Volcana says she's going after "the one with the claws" but blasts Storm instead. Magneto dodges the Absorbing Man and ends up tying Doctor Octopus's metal tentacles together.

Wolverine slices off Absorbing Man's right arm with his claws. An angry Volcana lashes out at Wolverine. Professor X orders Cyclops to stop her. His blast knocks her off-balance as Professor X confirms that Wolverine is still alive.

Rogue smacks Titania with a huge rock. With none of their tactics working, the villains make a run for it with Volcana providing cover.

This is one of the better-staged fights in the series. The artists do an excellent job of moving the characters around while keeping the storytelling clear and delivering a couple of visual shocks. Over the course of the nineteen-panel fight, almost every panel shows at least one character using their power with consequences, and with the heroes functioning as a team whenever possible. The visual of Absorbing Man losing his arm to Wolverine's claws is as effective as it is brutal.

At the end of the fight, the villains get away, but at least Xavier is philosophical. The X-Men have passed "our greatest

test to date" and "proved ourselves." Storm, however, still harbors doubts that Xavier is the best choice to lead them in combat.

Doctor Doom is still exploring Galactus's ship. The sensors in his armor "have led me to prize after prize … devices which, in the hands of a man as brilliant as myself, could provide power to conquer entire galaxies."

Sending Doctor Doom to Galactus's ship is a good story point. It's part of Doctor Doom's plan, but it also shows the reader the inside of the ship and how huge it is. Zeck gets a chance to draw a seemingly-small Doctor Doom against Galactus's giant equipment.

Galactus senses the trespass. He power-grabs Doctor Doom, encasing him in a field of Kirby Krackle, then tosses him from the ship.

Back at Doombase, the villains regroup with the wounded Molecule Man. Ultron says that "there are medical machines in the central infirmary" and that he can operate them, but not without orders from Doctor Doom. The Enchantress says that she could heal Molecule Man "for a price."

Absorbing Man works on his own science project, trying to reattach his arm. He decides to press it against the stump as he releases the properties of the rocks and transforms back to human. It's a painful process, but it works.

The Wrecking Crew struggles with the Lizard now that their "stasis-ray must'a worn off." Piledriver gets in a solid right, knocking him into a convenient holding cell. The Wrecking Crew then takes off for lunch, but Bulldozer wants a nap.

In his quarters, he feels a draft, because She-Hulk has knocked a hole in the wall and punches Bulldozer out for his part in killing Wasp. Zeck and Beatty really capture the fury of She-Hulk with action in the "mighty Marvel manner." It only takes a couple of punches before the rest of the Wrecking Crew responds. By the time Titania follows the noise, She-Hulk has taken care of the whole bunch.

Referring to Titania as "Doom's muscle-woman," She-Hulk gets in a couple of kicks before she's overwhelmed by Titania and the timely arrival of Doctor Octopus and Absorbing Man.

At the same time, Doctor Doom returns to Doombase, his armor battered from his fall from space. Like many characters in the series, he retreats to his bed to lie down, in full armor.

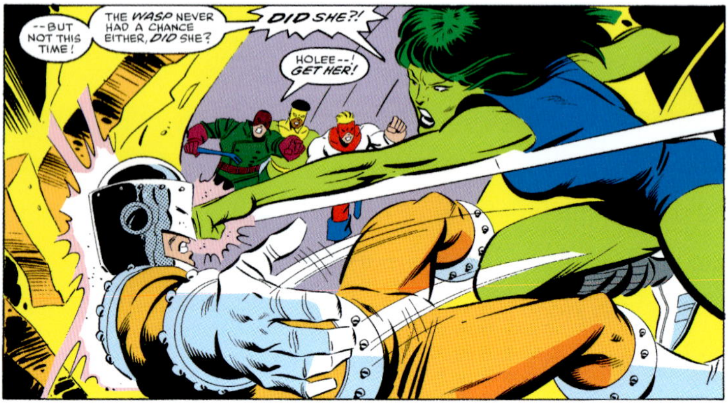

Hundreds of miles away, Cap, "a lonely man with the weight of all creation upon his shoulders," watches Galactus at work on his planet-eating machine. Hawkeye informs Cap that She-Hulk is missing. They all know where to find her. Cap wants to let them go, but there are "too many lives at stake here."

In Szaji's village, Colossus is not only up, he's also moving, looking for another treatment "so I can work and perhaps fight again!" He finds Zsaji coming out "of the hut where Wasp's body lies awaiting burial at dawn, if there is a dawn!" Zsaji drops to the ground, "so pale, barely breathing!"

The Zsaji storyline has to wait. Cap gets a telepathic communication from Xavier. The X-Men will stand watch over Galactus, freeing Cap and the others if, perhaps, they need to be elsewhere. Cap rallies the rest of his team to go after Doom with a cry of "Let's go get those butchers!"

The origin of Spider-Woman

The original version of Spider-Woman, created by Archie Goodwin and Marie Severin, debuted in *Marvel Spotlight* #32 (February 1977). Stan Lee appeared on a panel at James Madison University's Fine Arts Festival in March 1978. Asked about the creation of Spider-Woman, Lee said, "I suddenly realized that some other company may quickly put out a book like that and claim they have the right to use the name, and I thought we'd better do it real fast to copyright the name. So we just batted one quickly, and that's exactly what happened. I wanted to protect the name."

(From an appearance by Stan Lee at James Madison University's in 1978, reported in *The Comics Journal* #42 [October 1978])

The Marvel Age of Trivia

What is the Denver connection with Titania and Volcana? Why Denver? One of Jim Shooter's industry friends is Chuck Rozanski, the founder of Mile High Comics, which is based in—wait for it—Denver.

Barry Dutter

"Though she appears in shadow in the last panel of *Secret Wars* #6, *Secret Wars* #7 does feature the first in-costume appearance of Julia Carpenter, who became the second Spider-Woman. That issue typically sells for about $10 or less."

10

Marvel Super Heroes Secret Wars #8

"Invasion!"
Writer: Jim Shooter
Penciler: Mike Zeck
Inkers: John Beatty/Jack Abel/Mike Esposito
Letterer: Joe Rosen
Colorist: Christie Scheele
Editor: Tom DeFalco
Cover by Mike Zeck and John Beatty

This is the issue that everybody's been waiting for. Spider-Man had already appeared in his new black costume back in *Amazing Spider-Man* #252 in the same month as *Secret Wars* #1 seven months earlier. This, however, was the issue of *Secret Wars* that was going to explain how that happened. This is the marketing genius of the series, to have the

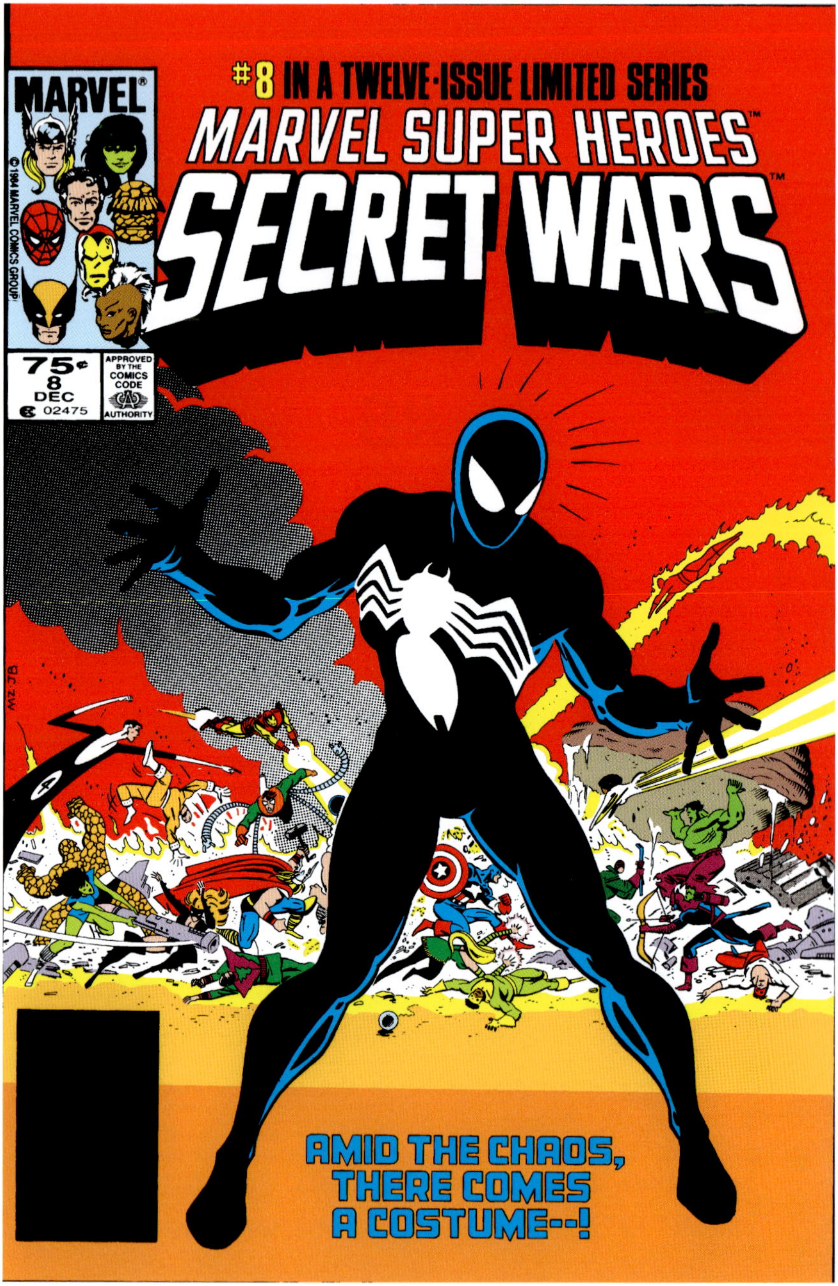
#8 IN A TWELVE-ISSUE LIMITED SERIES
MARVEL
MARVEL SUPER HEROES™
SECRET WARS™
© 1984 MARVEL COMICS GROUP
75¢
8
DEC
02475
APPROVED BY THE COMICS CODE AUTHORITY
AMID THE CHAOS, THERE COMES A COSTUME--!

change appear earlier but have the fans wait months for the explanation.

The schedule obviously hit a snag this month as Marvel stalwarts Jack Abel and Mike Esposito step in to do some credited support inking with series regular John Beatty.

The opening panel is a lot of fun as the heroes rush toward Doombase. Since they can't fly, Iron Man is again carrying a large flat rock that holds Spider-Woman, the Thing, Mr. Fantastic, Cap, and Hawkeye.

The X-Men have finally picked a side, and Cap thinks they can be trusted to keep an eye on Galactus. It's onward to Doombase to rescue She-Hulk and bash some bad guys. Doom hasn't detected their arrival, giving Thor time to toss Mjolnir into the side of Doombase, creating a hole for the heroes.

At Doombase, Enchantress has been downing flagons of self-conjured mead in her quarters and can barely stand up. She reveals her quest to obtain some hint from Thor that she could be his, and she can't decide if she will fight him or beg for his love.

Volcana also has her own man trouble, as her precious Owen recovers from his injuries. The Lizard, who was imprisoned in Doombase's "huge dungeon," has been freed by Klaw because he can't stand to see anyone trapped as he once was. She-Hulk has taken quite a beating from Doom's crew but Absorbing Man hears the noise of Thor's hammer.

Hulk embiggens the hole made by Mjolnir and the heroes enter Doombase. Captain Marvel takes off to look for She-Hulk. The fight is on.

Marvel's comics are known for their fight scenes and this one is particularly wild. It's the first fight where the heroes show up at Doombase. It's a much longer fight scene with the heroes motivated to rescue She-Hulk. Spider-Woman is also in her first real fight since joining the team last issue.

The Wrecker smacks Iron Man out of the air with his "super-duper crowbar." Iron Man uses his repulsor blast to send him "through the stinkin' wall." Doctor Octopus cracks open a convenient reservoir of water to douse the Human Torch. Spider-Man hits Bulldozer so hard his helmet pops off. The Thing confronts Absorbing Man before he can retaliate against Spider-Man. But the worst thing happens to the Thing. For no apparent reason (yet), he reverts to human form. "Whatta revoltin' development" that is!

Before Absorbing Man can use that to his advantage, Spider-Woman races in, picks him up and throws him into a metal wall. She double-taps him by hurling his own wrecking ball into his head.

Thor ties up Doctor Octopus with his own tentacles. Hawkeye shoots an incredulous Piledriver with an arrow. Piledriver stumbles away, arrow in his shoulder, grumbling like a delicate snowflake.

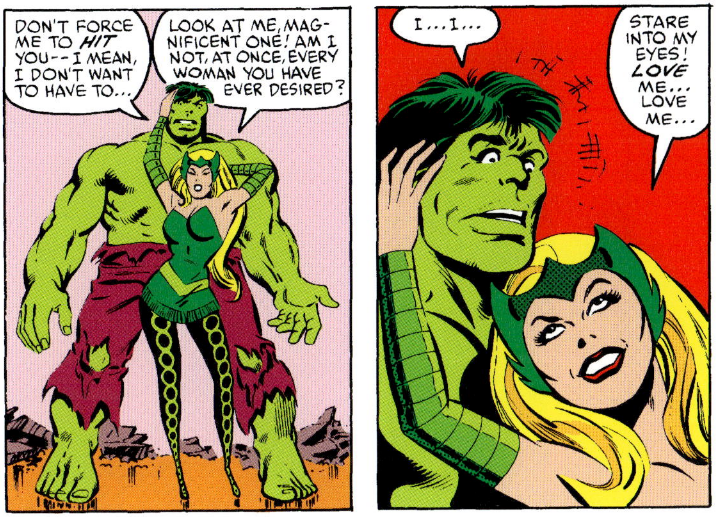

Hulk punches through another wall and into the Enchantress's bedroom. She uses her cozy up powers, enchanting him until he passes out like a "mortal cretin."

Cap enters the room, and Enchantress tries the same trick. "I am yours, handsome Captain! Am I not beautiful? Come to me!" But Cap can't be suckered, so she tries to blast him. Cap is too tricky and athletic. With a couple of quick flips, he bashes a disbelieving Enchantress in the face with his shield. Vibranium for the win, as she falls unconscious.

In the Doombase infirmary, Volcana hears the fight moving closer. "The first one who shows his face through that door's getting crispy-fried!" Molecule Man has awoken and he wants to help his darling Marsha: "We'll annihilate them!"

Iron Man, Reed, Thor, and Spider-Woman enter the infirmary and are blasted back. Iron Man claims he'll "roust their butts outta there!" He doesn't get the chance. Volcana blasts him directly with "plasma-generated heat."

Mr. Fantastic pulls Iron Man out of the way. Captain Marvel explains to Molecule Man that his protective shield isn't invisible, "it's transparent." That means Captain Marvel can just walk in and put a chokehold on Owen.

Volcana powers down and surrenders because Owen has fainted, and his wounds have reopened. Captain Marvel loosens her grip on Owen.

Titania crashes down the I-beam on Spider-Man, but he spider-powers his way out of danger. Spider-Man air-flips

Ditko-style, kicks Titania into a wall, punches her in the face, double-punches her, then tosses her out of Doombase to the rocks below.

Shooter makes sure that all the heroes and villains get fight time at locations throughout Doombase.

Ultron finally makes an appearance and gets a stranglehold on Torch's neck. Cap urges him to "use your Nova-Flame!" Cap hides behind his shield for protection, and again Vibranium for the win.

Cap finds Doctor Doom and this is "how it ought to be." Doctor Doom is still too weak to battle, and Cap pronounces him "harmless."

In one of the funniest scenes in the entire series, Hawkeye and Ben Grimm have defeated Klaw temporarily by playing patty-cake with him. This causes the Lizard to exclaim to Reed, "Dissssturb our gamess-s and the Lizard will desstroy you!" The Lizard says they'll surrender once the game is over.

It's the silliest bit in the storyline, and the visual of Ben and Klaw sitting cross-legged on the floor of Doombase patty-caking should bring a smile to even the most serious Marvel fan.

This little bit of humor helps to break up the seriousness of the fight. It also proves that not every battle is a fistfight or a powerblast.

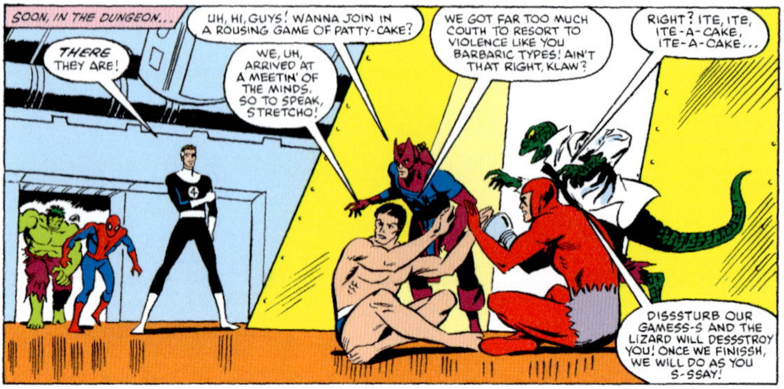

Meanwhile, Captain Marvel has found the wounded She-Hulk, unconscious and in rough shape. In the infirmary of Doombase, the wounded from both sides—including She-Hulk—are placed into individual healing chambers.

Cap feels guilty about the choices he's made so far, and that "if I'd done things differently" the Wasp might still be alive. Reed lets him off the hook, saying, "No one could have led us better or more wisely."

There's still Wasp's body to deal with. Hawkeye wants her "to have a proper burial … worthy of an Avenger."

In the alien village, Colossus carries the unconscious body of Szaji to her home. He's still clearly smitten with her, calling her "lovely one." He sees the bottle that the Human Torch told him about. It's "the one containing vapors which link minds."

Colossus opens the bottle, letting the vapors out. They do their smoky work and reveal the truth to Colossus: Wasp is

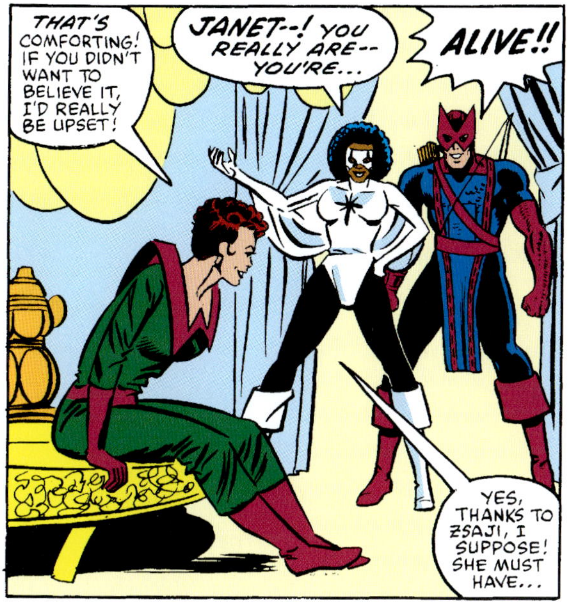

not dead, merely wounded, and in some kind of "death-like stasis!"

At Doombase, the rest of the team is in for a shock as Wasp jolts upright.

Reed uses "advanced alien technology" to not only patch Iron Man's armor but "make it far better than it was." Iron Man asks if Reed was "surprised there was a Black man under the metal." Reed replies with one of the great Marvel lines of this era: "No, I never gave it a thought. I knew there was a *man* under there."

Marvel has been consistently progressive in dealing with

issues of race in their comics. There's a throughline of anti-racism that has been explicit in places like *Sgt. Fury And His Howling Commandos* #6 (1964), the work of Don McGregor's *Black Panther* and *Killraven*, and the diverse casts of several other titles. Here, Shooter tackles it with a bit of subtlety, gets the point across, and moves on.

The issue's almost over and Spider-Man hasn't obtained his new costume yet. It's coming. The web-slinger runs into Thor and the Hulk. Thor has a new cape and helmet.

The Hulk describes a machine where "you just think into it and it produces any sort of cloth or clothing you want." Spider-Man is excited about getting some "new threads."

Unfortunately, Spider-Man forgot to ask which of the many machines was the magic clothing device. He picks one that looks like it might do the job, and it releases a small black glob. The glob expands, crawling up Spider-Man's arm, quickly creating a black spider-suit that snugly covers his body. New costume achievement unlocked!

It's a very dynamic scene, but given the scope of the overall story, it's also a relatively small moment. However, its impact on the Marvel Universe as a whole would be wide-ranging. It is precisely changes like this that set the foundation for other Marvel creators to build the new costume into a major element in other stories and turn the black suit into a separate fan-favorite character and movie star.

The new suit sets the template for the big event comics that will follow after *Secret Wars.* In order to attract reader interest and to create future storylines for post-event continuity, these kinds of blockbusters need to have one or more changes including new characters, new relationships, deaths, costumes, and more. By being first, *Secret Wars* established key story elements that readers expect and anticipate in other events.

While the new Spider-Man costume would have the greatest influence, other changes would eventually spill out of *Secret Wars.* There will be a new line-up for the Fantastic Four, and a change in the relationship between Colossus and his beloved Kitty Pryde.

Spider-Man doesn't get time to enjoy his new costume before the ground shakes violently, like "a planetquake!" Xavier telepathically contacts the heroes: "It has begun! Galactus is devouring the planet!"

Eighties TV reference

Piledriver tells Hawkeye he'll soon need "Hawkeye the M*A*S*H doctor."

Stan Lee on Spider-Man's new costume

"Well, they're running a special series of stories, called The Marvels, *Secret Wars*. Involving most of our super heroes and villains, in one fantastic series. Which will extend over 12 issues.

And for the purpose of that series, they've changed the colors of Spider-Man's costume. And it has to do with something in the story. The reasons for that will be made clear towards the end of the story.

And, in fact, that series has been so incredibly successful, I believe Mattel is doing a whole toy line, based on it. And I think we're going to then do a second series. But eventually, the costume will change back to the original one.

Although there may be times when this new black costume reappears. Which is probably the most confusing answer I've ever given."

(Stan Lee on WOR Radio's *Good Afternoon New York*, June 22, 1984)

Danny Fingeroth

"I think Jim Shooter came to me with the designs by Mike Zeck for the black Spider-Man costume. (I later found out

it was inspired by a cold submission from an artist who Jim paid a fee to for the idea.) Probably also the designs for the new Spider-Woman, too, since their costumes were variants on each other.

Amazing Spider-Man was wrapping up the Hobgoblin storyline, and transitioning between writers—Roger Stern to Tom DeFalco—so it was reasonably simple to incorporate the symbiote costume into the storyline. John Romita Jr. had moved to the *X-Men*, so after the costume's introduction in *ASM* #252, we had two issues penciled by Rick Leonardi to buy Ron Frenz time to get up to speed as regular penciler, which is why there are those sketches around that Rick did with small modifications on the costume, and why some people think he designed it.

Incorporating the black costume into *Spectacular Spider-Man* was a fairly smooth process, too. But *Marvel Team-Up* had had a fill-in scheduled for its first issue with the black costume, so that title's black costume debut feels a little more shoehorned in, because it was.

And, since Spider-Man was in three monthly titles, parsing out bits and pieces of the black costume saga between all three titles was somewhat complicated. We wanted to reward people who bought all three titles, but not penalize anyone who didn't."

Randy Schueller

"Back in the early '80s, Marvel ran a competition for aspiring writers and artists. Being a life long Spidey fan with delusions of comic grandeur, I took a stab at a story idea. I saw the new suit as a stealth version of the original costume—jet black so he could blend in with the shadows. A few months after submitting the story I received a letter from Jim Shooter saying he liked the idea and wanted to buy it for $220. I was thrilled!"

(*Comic Book Resources*, May 16, 2007, interview by Brian Cronin, "Comic Book Urban Legends Revealed")

Jim Shooter

"The correspondent sent in a sample plot in which Spider-Man is given a new, black costume by Reed Richards that has high-tech features. His plot wasn't up to professional standards, but I offered to pay him for it anyway, to 'buy the idea.' A long time later, maybe a year, I needed an event for *Secret Wars* and remembered the black costume idea. I thought it would be a throwaway bit, something we'd use once."

(JimShooter.com, September 9, 2011)

Tom Brevoort

"From personal experience, I can remember how I felt when it was first announced that Spidey was getting a new costume coming out of *Secret Wars*. It was the stupidest thing I'd ever heard! Spidey's costume is a classic, the new, black design wasn't in keeping with the character, and it was an alien super-costume to boot! I wasn't reading Spidey at the time (having stopped just a few months prior to that), but I was nonetheless outraged–how dare Marvel ruin this classic character that I loved? Of course now, that outfit itself is a classic, and is effortlessly accepted as part of the overall tapestry of Spidey's life. A reader who began following Spidey even as much as twenty years ago never even knew a Spidey who didn't have one. And that string of stories by

Tom DeFalco and Ron Frenz look pretty good in hindsight as well."
(TomBrevoort.com, April 18, 2021)
(In the years since *Secret Wars*, Brevoort became Executive Editor and Senior Vice President of Publishing at Marvel Comics.)

Barry Dutter

"*Secret Wars* #8 is one of the most coveted comics of the past 40 years. It's often referred to as the first appearance of the black costume, but that is not quite right. *Amazing Spider-Man* #252 is the book that featured the debut of Spidey's new black suit. *ASM* #252 had a cover date of May 1984. And *Secret Wars* #8 had a cover date of December 1984. If you go on eBay, you will see many sellers offering *Secret Wars* #8 as the 'first appearance of the black costume' and technically they are correct. But those who list *ASM* #252 as the first appearance are correct as well."

Stan Lee

(On writing the *Spider-Man* comic strip.)
"It isn't tough at all because I don't coordinate it. I just write my script as if there is no comic book and they do the comic book as if there's no strip."
(*Comics Buyer's Guide*, July 3, 1987, interview by John Weber)

11

Marvel Super Heroes Secret Wars #9

"Assault On Galactus!"
Writer: Jim Shooter
Penciler: Mike Zeck
Inkers: John Beatty/Jack Abel/Mike Esposito
Letterer: Joe Rosen
Colorist: Christie Scheele
Editor: Tom DeFalco
Cover by Mike Zeck and Bob McLeod

Responding to the "planetquake," Colossus races out of Zsaji's hut with the exclamation, "Galactus has begun to devour the planet!"

Colossus runs back to Zsaji's side to say a sad farewell and also admit his love for her: "I did not truly know beauty, nobility and selfless compassion until I met you." Colossus

#9 IN A TWELVE-ISSUE LIMITED SERIES
MARVEL SUPER HEROES
SECRET WARS
MARVEL
© 1984 MARVEL COMICS GROUP
75¢
9
JAN
02475
APPROVED BY THE COMICS CODE AUTHORITY

bounces from his feelings of love towards Kitty Pryde back on Earth, and his instant feelings of love towards Zsaji.

High above Galactus's mountain, Storm gathers clouds together and brings down the sky's fury onto Galactus and his planet-devouring device. Magneto points out that "he seemed not to notice."

Xavier, still in slacks and a white shirt, tells everyone that they are in "combat communications mode," which probably didn't exist until this issue. He will give "all orders telepathically! You must obey instantly!"

Rogue picks up where Storm leaves off. Galactus materializes what looks like "a cosmic flyswatter," according to Nightcrawler. When Nightcrawler is swatted away, Xavier calls an audible: "Cyclops! Full-force optic blast on my command! Strike!"

The subsequent explosion on the mountain is huge. It's witnessed by Hawkeye, Wasp, and Captain Marvel from the village below. They're pretty sure it was the X-Men who were up there. If so, Captain Marvel says, "they're dead for sure!" Obviously, she's never read a Marvel comic.

Cap's team assembles in Doombase and takes off in the skyjet. The journey becomes a mild therapy session. Thor tries to bond with a pouty Hulk. He's worried that he's "not savage enough or smart enough to be a relevant factor" in the fight that's coming.

Ben wishes he could "change back 'n' forth" like the Torch.

Striking his fist on a console, Ben regains his rockpile form and changes back into the Thing. He's so ecstatic, he hugs the Human Torch. "I'm so happy, I even like you!"

Iron Man's eager to use his souped-up armor, to show everyone that "Jim Rhodes is Iron Man, now and forever!"

It's black-costumed Spider-Man who is the most playful of them all. Not only does he have a new costume, "I've got my webs back!" He demonstrates by webbing the Human Torch in the face.

Reed cannibalized Spider-Man's web-shooters earlier in the series, but these new ones are part of the suit. "They fire when I think about it," Spider-Man exclaims. That's not all. The new suit can make instant fashion adjustments. In a flash, Spider-Man's new costume has short pants and short sleeves "for summer." He looks less like a super hero and more like a masked bike messenger.

Reed knows that Galactus must be the key, but before he can take his thoughts further, their skyjet is hit.

They're too low and they're going to crash. The ship is saved from disaster by the arrival of Colossus. He "catches" the ship like it was a fat watermelon and brings it to the surface, working in conjunction with the ship's "retros" and "auto-stabilizers."

Shooter is very good at staging the super-battles at different locations in each issue. It creates fight-diversity in the visuals, and it gives Zeck and Beatty different environments to draw. In this issue, the team is fighting uphill to the top of Galactus's mountain.

Galactus's machine sends out power-tendrils to rip the planet apart. The group has only seconds "before the world-burn starts!" With no time to waste, Cap leads the team up the mountain toward Galactus. Defense drones try to stop them, but Iron Man is able to avoid them thanks to his upgrades and "in-flight dodging computers."

Watching the fight, Reed has an epiphany. They must *not* stop Galactus! If they let Galactus win this contest, and if the Beyonder keeps his word, Galactus will no longer be planet-hungry "at long last!"

If the Beyonder doesn't pay up? Then Galactus will be destroyed trying to force the Beyonder's hand. It's win-win for the universe. Spider-Man poses the most interesting question: "Why us?"

Reed has a great answer: "We beings of Earth seem to have a knack for being pivotal in the cosmic scheme of things." This is just about the best summary of life in the Marvel Universe, and it's tossed out almost casually by one of the smartest Marvel heroes. From deep underground with the Mole Man, to the vast reaches of space with Thanos, Silver Surfer, Star-Lord, and so many others, Marvel Earth plays a constant role in the cosmos.

This is an explanation that Marvel creators can use to explain any story they develop. Earth has a role in the galaxy and beyond. Anything a writer can imagine comes with a ready-made explanation. Shooter has already set down the reasoning here for future reference.

Before Reed can explain any more, he's teleported to Galactus's home. He stretches his way through the corridors with wide-eyed wonder. Galactus's residence "pulses with life, with living splendor!" He's obviously overwhelmed.

As soon as Reed reaches Galactus sitting in his favorite chair, Galactus projects an image of Reed's homelife for him to see. There's little Franklin and wife Sue, who is still pregnant. A joyous Reed says, "She hasn't had the baby yet!"

Meanwhile, Doctor Doom sits in a maximum security containment room inside Doombase, where the heroes left him. Doctor Doom realizes that "Galactus's home itself is the way I seek!" He's got to get out "before opportunity evades" his grasp!

Fortunately, Doom "is ever prepared." He presses a hidden button in his right boot and blows the door off his cell. He ignores the pleas of his fellow villains for similar release because "I have no use for you now … save one!" That one is, obviously, Klaw.

Doctor Doom has a plan for Klaw: "I'm going to dissect you!"

At the mountain where the X-Men attacked Galactus, a frantic Colossus digs through the rubble, looking for his comrades. He's nearly bisected by an optic blast from underground as the X-Men emerge! They're alive!

That's because Magneto pulled "a thick layer of earth and stone" over them. They join Cap and the others at the village. Zsaji finally awakens, and runs right to the Human Torch, calling out "Jah-nee! Jah-nee!"

Cap, the Hulk, and Captain Marvel toss out ideas for how

to take out Galactus, and surprisingly the Thing is the voice of reason. "Reed said not to fight Galactus, so we ain't gonna!"

They're interrupted by the arrival of Galactus setting up his device again on the mountain.

That's enough for Cap. He rallies the heroes to his side because "I'm going to fight!" He thanks Xavier for his support and invites the X-Men and Magneto to join him.

Doctor Doom has other priorities, while "there is still time!" For some reason, the Beyonder "has opened his portal again." Possibly he "senses the awesome significance of the next few moments."

In the creepiest panel yet in the series, Klaw lays on an

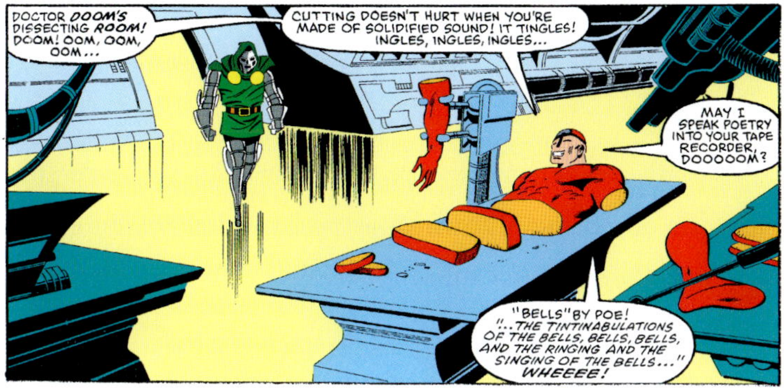

operating table, partially dissected into slices, as if Doctor Doom ran a horror movie deli. Klaw has even created a rhyme, calling the lab "Doctor Doom's Dissecting Room."

As a writer, Shooter generally sticks to lofty themes in the battle of good and evil, of heroes rising up, and people doing the right thing. What he is not known for is comedy. Yet in this series, he seems to be having a blast with the revitalized Klaw and his goofy rhymes and silly observations. Zeck seems inspired to put Klaw in poses that make him look like a marionette.

Galactus stands tall as the heroes approach. He successfully blasts them back. Reed tells the Human Torch to hit at Galactus, then has Ben undercut the mountain to sever the "anchor rods and probe wands" that stabilize the machine.

Reed believes that because Galactus has "used enormous

amounts of energy transporting his homeworld here," it means he hasn't eaten a planet in months. His power "is almost depleted."

Galactus jets off into the sky, back towards his world-ship. He starts devouring his own ship, "perhaps the greatest energy source in the universe." Once finished, and fully powered, he's going to devour Battleworld, and "maybe the sun, too." He'll need all that energy to take on the Beyonder. Reed's closing words are: "we're dead men."

In Doctor Doom's lab, he has fashioned lenses from Klaw's body "singularly attuned to the energy of the world-ship." He's going to steal Galactus's power and draw it to himself.

It's so crazy, it just might work!

Hello Spider-Woman!

In this issue, Iron Man calls Spider-Woman "the new broad" and says "she's got great legs!"

Jim Shooter

"Would you believe that Stan Lee called me the other day and said 'Jim, I gotta know—how does it end?'"

(*Comics Interview* #14, 1984, interview by Jim Salicrup)

Mike Zeck

"Every issue had its own set of problems to make the shipping date. I know Tom DeFalco and the rest of the crew that worked on it will agree that it was amazing that we got the books out on schedule. It was nightmarish, but somehow we managed to do it."

(*Comics Interview* #72, 1989, interview by Renée Witterstaetter)

12

Marvel Super Heroes Secret Wars #10

"Death To The Beyonder!"
Writer: Jim Shooter
Penciler: Mike Zeck
Inkers: John Beatty
Letterer: Joe Rosen
Colorist: Christie Scheele
Editor: Tom DeFalco
Cover by Mike Zeck and Terry Austin

The issue leads off with an iconic cover. It's a battered, beaten Doctor Doom, bleeding, down on one knee, fists at the ready. It's a terrific illustration by Mike Zeck, masterfully inked by Terry Austin. It's Austin's first and only credited work on the series.

Galactus's world-ship is being devoured by Galactus. There's

MARVEL
© 1984 MARVEL COMICS GROUP
75¢
10
FEB
02475
APPROVED BY THE COMICS CODE AUTHORITY
#10 IN A TWELVE-ISSUE LIMITED SERIES
MARVEL SUPER HEROES
SECRET WARS
AGAINST THE BEYONDER. . . TO THE DEATH!

a great panel at the top of page 2 showing the skeletal forms of the heroes as they're bathed in the after-effects. It's imaginative and jarring at the same time.

Quickly, "the last remains of the enormous world-ship are transformed, swelling the nimbus of raw energy." Galactus is about to "drink deep" of the energy, but it's suddenly ripped from him.

The heroes note that the energy is heading straight to Doombase. Captain Marvel turns "her body to pure electromagnetic radiation" and heads there.

Once inside, she finds Doom laying on a slab underneath a massive machine. She correctly deduces that "it looks like he's using it to draw all that energy into himself!" Xavier telepathically links Captain Marvel to Reed because "he is best qualified to interpret for us the meaning and significance of the events" that she's witnessing.

Doom is done, though. "The power is mine!"

The effects of Doom absorbing the power are a brilliant blend of line art and coloring. The energy comes through on the page, and there's an added smattering of "Kirby Krackle" on page 4.

Shooter has provided the series with a large number of unique visual moments that demonstrate the power of the characters. From the Beyonder destroying a galaxy and creating a world, to Doctor Doom getting tossed from Galactus's ship, to Galactus trying to eat Battleworld and then his own ship, to this scene of Doom stealing Galactus's power, Shooter has given Zeck, Layton, Beatty, and Scheele interesting challenges. The team rises to the occasion.

Doom feels "every cell, every atom!" No physical barrier can restrain his senses. He's even aware that there's a spy within Doombase. Captain Marvel's link to Xavier is cut.

The heroes need to rush to her aid, but their ship was damaged in the fight against Galactus. With their other ship wrecked, too, whatever will they do?

Magneto orders everyone to get into the ship because "I am the power!" Using his magnetism, Magneto flies the ship even faster than if it had a working engine.

Since Xavier vouched for Magneto, Cap has "no qualms about him or the rest of the mutants."

Wolverine is offended. He brings up that the "mutants are

at war!" He points out that Cap is only interested in humans. He just stands by "while mutants are being persecuted" and has never "fought for our rights!"

Wolverine continues: "Some of the god-fearin' Americans you protect hate mutants, and when they come after us, it's a lot like how the Nazis went after the Jews!"

This is heavy stuff for Shooter to drop in the middle of a massive battle. It solidifies the X-Men story as a metaphor for oppressed groups around the world.

Wolverine says that Magneto has chosen a direct approach of fighting back, while Xavier wants "us to hide, try to help humanity, earn acceptance, fit in!" Wolverine wonders if Magneto's approach might be right.

Cap says that "nothing justifies terrorism, or murder." Wolverine ends the conversation with a very tight rebuke: "Terrorists? That's what the big army calls the little army! I used to have some respect for you!"

At Doombase, Doom realizes the Beyonder's portal remains open, an obvious sign that "these are critical moments." Doom recognizes that there is only one enemy "in all existence worthy" of himself. That's the Beyonder. According to Doom, "as long as I knew there was one greater, I could never rest!"

Doom knows that he's the David to the Beyonder's Goliath, but he has a trick up his armored sleeve. During Doom's initial attack on the Beyonder's portal back in issue #1, the computers in his armor "analyzed his energies." Using that data, Doom makes "a few simple adjustments." He mixes that with "some technology from the device Galactus meant to use to absorb the energy of the planet."

Suddenly, in three panels, Doctor Doom now has a new costume. His armor is sleeker and leaner, and his cape is gone. He's ready.

He bids farewell to severed-head Klaw.

Just in time, too, as the heroes burst into Doombase. Xavier telepathically traces Klaw to the lab. There, Spider-Woman and the others find a frozen Captain Marvel and severed-head Klaw.

Severed-head Klaw says that Doctor Doom will be right back. "He's using some gadget in this chestplate to steal all The Beyonder's power and conquer him!"

Cap says that Doom "must be insane!" Severed-head Klaw agrees, noting, "maybe that's why we get along!"

Doctor Doom is already at the Beyonder's portal, energy crackling around him. The Beyonder, who hasn't spoken in quite a while, tells Doom "you cannot approach me!" He calls the Beyonder a coward, proclaims himself master, and demands that he "grovel before Doom!"

Let the battle begin!

Doombase is shaken and tossed around by Doctor Doom's attack on the Beyonder.

Reed stretches to a working monitor. He can see the source of the disturbance at the Beyonder's portal. There's no time to soup up the equipment to see what's inside the portal, but it can still be used to "locate Galactus" so that Reed can bring him back to Doombase to "help him, revitalize him." Sure, the planet-eater might try to kill them all again, but if Doctor Doom ends his attack on the Beyonder, he might turn his attention to the heroes. They'd need the "power of Galactus" on their side.

Throughout the series, Shooter has kept alliances fluid and constantly shifting. This is a very clever way to keep the characters off-balance and propel the story forward. Different dynamics can reveal both character and relationships. Shifting allegiances can move the plot in unexpected directions.

Reed spots the helpless Galactus floating in space and locks a tractor beam onto his coordinates. Doombase is rattled yet again, shaking loose the monitor which falls on top of Reed, flattening him underneath. The Thing lifts it off, but Reed can't catch his breath.

Colossus sees that Zsaji is hurt, so naturally he mopes, "If only I were there to be with you now!" Colossus knows that, sadly, she prefers the Human Torch. As Johnny comforts the injured Reed, he says he's "got no time for a chippie! … I'll send her a card later!" Ladies, take note. That's what Johnny's "love" is worth.

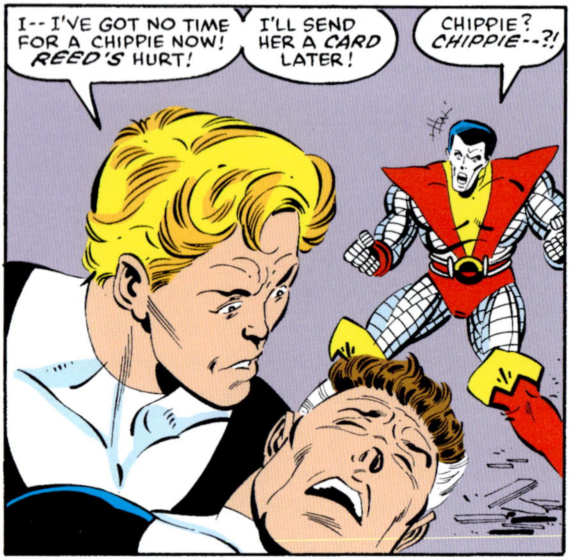

Another shockwave bounces the team around Doombase. The battle between Doctor Doom and the Beyonder has kicked into a higher gear. The aggressive ego of Doctor Doom is taking a beating: "All my power is not enough!"

Before Doctor Doom has a chance to figure out a new plan, the Beyonder's powers cut off his left leg above the knee. Doctor Doom falls to the ground with a very melodramatic "thus falls Doom?"

Doctor Doom will not "fall prey to the very spectre of death." He will deny her because "Victor Von Doom must not die!"

There is momentary quiet within Doombase. Its remains "shiver and settle." Inside the lab, Xavier issues a warning that "something is approaching!" Even Spider-Man's Spider-Sense "is going bazonkers!"

They are both correct.

Doctor Doom suddenly appears between all the heroes, only now he's in some kind of astral form. He has "transcended mortality" (and gotten his leg back, at least in this form). He claims to be the group's champion, "fighting for your sakes!" He says he's "about to crush the Beyonder" because "he is the real enemy!"

According to Doctor Doom, "I, Doom, have dared to attack the Beyonder" and that it's "gone well." He says the Beyonder "cringes in terror, marshaling his failing strength against my final assault." There's no proof of this, however.

The real purpose of Doctor Doom's visit to the heroes is to make a request. He wants them to "share in my glorious conquest!" If they lend him their own power, it will "hasten his certain defeat!" All they have to do is touch his hand. After it's all over, he shall grant "power beyond measure" to help them pursue their own "noble purposes!"

They're all shocked—except for Magneto, who rushes to gladly accept Doctor Doom's offer. He hesitates, locking eyes briefly with Xavier. Then, before he can grab Doctor Doom's hand, Magneto is tackled by Hawkeye and Iron Man, and stung by the Wasp. Iron Man gets in the best line: "He ain't gonna reach out and touch nobody unless he can find a pay phone!"

Doctor Doom can no longer maintain his form and fades away. Magneto is furious that the "human scum" have dared to interfere. Iron Man says there's "no way we're lettin' you help Doom!"

Cap claims "we were all tempted" by Doctor Doom's offer. He suspects that Doctor Doom "was exerting some sort of mental control, and maybe Magneto got the biggest dose." Cap saw that Magneto stopped himself, which means "he did nothing wrong!"

Nobody at Doombase knows what's happening out there by the portal, and Cap thinks "it's possible we'll regret not helping Doom!"

The battle between Doctor Doom and the Beyonder has started up again. It seems to end quickly, with Doctor Doom unconscious on the ground. He's still missing his leg, but now also his left arm from above the elbow is gone as well. This isn't going well for Doctor Doom as the Beyonder "begins to probe," finding "the apparent center of its fallen foe's being!"

The origin of Doctor Doom then unfolds, as the Beyonder "sees before him the life-journey of this carrion he holds." There's young Doom as "a gypsy youth, handsome and proud"; Doctor Doom's mother, "the healer, maker of potions" who was "slain for failing to cure an ailing horse"; his discovery of "his mother's hidden cache of sorcerous and scientific secrets"; and that once he tried to contact her spirit in "an infernal, extra-dimensional netherworld" and ended up with his face "a scarred ruin."

This is an unexpected twist that adds quite a bit of depth to Doctor Doom's character. No villain ever sees themselves as bad, and many of Doctor Doom's motivations can be traced to his relationship with his murdered mother and anger at her death.

Following this origin, the Beyonder then discovers "the desires which rule this shattered man." Those desires are simple: "control over the destinies of other men," "freedom for his mother's spirit," and "restoration of his ravaged face." There is more for the Beyonder to discover. He mentally dissects Doctor Doom's body, "leaving one side intact for comparison."

Doctor Doom awakens, "feeling half of his body being peeled apart, peeled away in layers."

> "The agony, the nausea, and the horror are beyond imagining. Utter death, only split-seconds away, offers an escape, which any other mortal would gratefully accept, but he is Doom! The breastplate hovers near, and the Beyonder himself is close at hand! His remaining arm quivers weakly, its battered flesh loathe to respond, but he is Doom!"

This is some of Shooter's most evocative writing on the series. It's very pulpy and fully comics, especially Marvel

Comics from the 1970s as written by newcomers Don McGregor, Chris Claremont, and Doug Moench.

Shooter delivers a gut-wrenching account of the Beyonder probing Doctor Doom's mind. It sets a high bar for future event comics to try to reach. It also manages, however briefly, to create some sympathy for Marvel's greatest villain as he appears lost and at the mercy of the Beyonder.

The page ends with the naked, dissected Doom reaching his right arm towards his armor that's floating towards him.

Over at Doombase, the entire place is "coming down" as a result of the battle. As the building crumbles, Cap orders the heroes outside and to safety. Cap remains behind momentarily and, with an assist from Wolverine, frees the villains from their cells. Wolverine wasn't "going to let these men die in cages, no matter what they done or whose side they're on!"

Cap agrees that "even these men have rights!" Wolverine and Cap even come to a healthy understanding of each other. Wolverine tells Cap, "I'm an attacker an' you're a defender, but we're both soldiers."

In a full-page splash, a kaiju-sized Doctor Doom appears, fully healed in his newer armor. The giant Doctor Doom has a major issue-ending announcement: "The Beyonder is dead! Now, the supreme being in the universe is Doom!"

The final page is two panels. The first is a reaction shot of the heroes all looking up towards the off-panel giant Doctor Doom.

Cap warns that "this is going to be the fight of our lives" and "we must find a way, we will find a way to win!"

A seemingly-friendlier Doctor Doom returns to human proportions to offer up a stunning revelation: "The Beyonder no longer exists, and Doom has been reborn! Thus have two evils come to an end."

Doctor Doom takes off his faceplate, revealing his face for the first time and proclaiming that "the war is over!" The audience can't see Doom's face yet. It's a great cliffhanger, but there are still two issues left in the series, so perhaps the war isn't over yet at all.

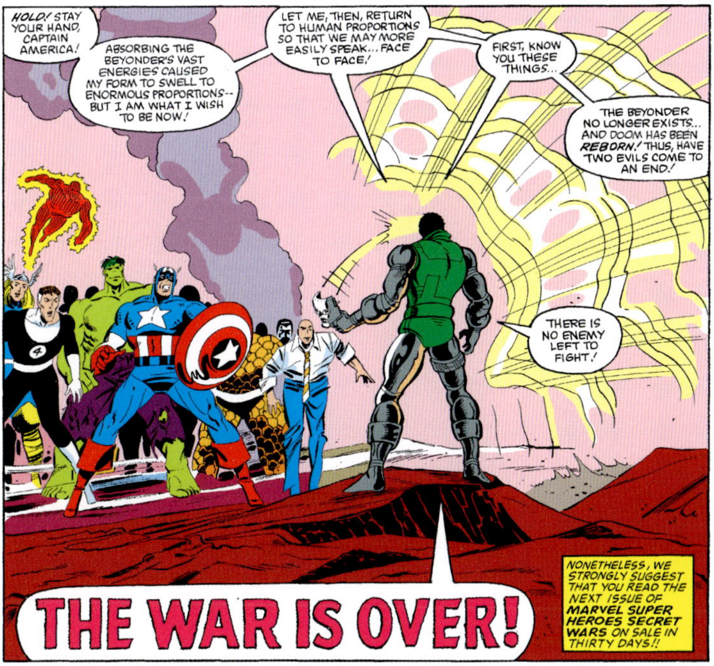

The Marvel Age of Biblical References

Doctor Doom invokes the story of David and Goliath.

Old advertising slogan

"Reach Out And Touch Someone" was a popular slogan for AT&T in the 1970s and 1980s.

Jim Shooter

"As long as people care about the characters as much as you care about the characters, you've succeeded. You've communicated."

(*Comics Interview* #14, 1984, interview by Jim Salicrup)

13

Marvel Super Heroes Secret Wars #11

"... And Dust To Dust!"
Writer: Jim Shooter
Penciler: Mike Zeck
Inkers: John Beatty
Letterer: Joe Rosen
Colorist: Nelson Yomtov
Editor: Tom DeFalco
Cover by Mike Zeck

In a shocking twist, Doctor Doom has removed his iron faceplate and revealed the human underneath.

The twist-on-the-twist is that it's not Doctor Doom's real face, which had been a Marvel secret for many years. It's just a version of his face that's been remade and fresh-scrubbed by Doctor Doom's new powers.

#11 IN A TWELVE-ISSUE LIMITED SERIES
MARVEL®
MARVEL SUPER HEROES™
SECRET WARS™
© 1984 MARVEL COMICS GROUP
75¢
11
MAR
02475
APPROVED BY THE COMICS CODE AUTHORITY
THE FACE OF DOOM

While new-face Doom chats amiably with the heroes, his villainous cronies jump to the conclusion that they've "always been disposable—pawns to be exploited and sacrificed." They're ready to unleash their anger at Doctor Doom's apparent betrayal.

Molecule Man sends the heroes away. He is ready to take on Doctor Doom himself, saying "I'm going to obliterate you!" Doctor Doom isn't impressed. He offers to show Molecule Man that he's even more powerful than he realizes.

Placing his hands directly on Molecule Man's forehead, Doctor Doom gives Owen "a gift: insight into the intricate simplicity of existence." Molecule Man is ready to take over leadership of the group of villains. Volcana suggests they all "go to my place, Owie!"

The villains gather in the "modest apartment of Marsha Rosenberg, aka Volcana." Zeck and Beatty prove themselves capable of drawing characters just sitting around a living room with the same skill they use for super-fights.

It's a good plot move meant to sideline the villains and narrowcast the focus of the upcoming final issue toward the heroes, Doctor Doom, and the Beyonder.

The villains would like to go home. The master of all the molecules encases the Denver suburb in a protective bubble. He lifts the suburb out of Battleworld and starts its journey back to Earth.

Cap suggests that the heroes get some sleep at Doombase and "try to figure this all out in the morning." Sleep proves difficult for Colossus, however, because he has switched from moping about his relationship with Kitty Pryde to moping about his supposed relationship with Zsaji, the alien healer. Colossus crushes hard.

Colossus steals away and heads off to the village to proclaim his love. As he leaves, "a small flickering point of radiance" streaks toward Doombase.

The "radiance" taps into the sleeping Hulk and takes control of him. One panel later, Hulk heads down the hall where he encounters Spider-Woman. The radiance transfers to her. She continues down the corridor and, "like a hunter seeking prey," enters Doctor Doom's lab. She goes past the frozen form of Captain Marvel and the sleeping severed-head Klaw before she's bathed in a flash of yellow light.

Her scream awakens Cap and the others. By the time they arrive in Doctor Doom's lab to see Spider-Woman, they also discover Doctor Doom left a message carved into a wall: "You are summoned to the Tower of Doom at dusk tomorrow."

Colossus shows up in Zsaji's home with a bouquet of freshly picked alien flowers. He tries hard to communicate with her before finally just blurting out, "I love you, Zsaji!"

Eighteen hours pass and it's almost time for the heroes to head to the Tower of Doom. Colossus still hasn't returned yet from his special night with Zsaji. That gives Wolverine the opportunity to bub-splain relationships to Nightcrawler. According to Wolverine, Colossus can't see that "this obsession of his is just a side effect of her healing power."

The heroes gather and it's a short flight to Doctor Doom's new hangout. Klaw takes them to see him and he can't wait to monologue about his new powers.

According to Doom, now that he's killed the Beyonder and absorbed all his power, he's no longer interested in the petty revenge schemes, world domination plans, and greedy power grabs of his earlier self. To prove his new heartwarming reality, he uses his new powers to not only bring Kang back to life, but also to send him back "to his home."

Doctor Doom reports that he's arranged for Galactus to be aided by his herald, the female Nova. With all that accomplished, he is ready to grant Cap and the others a chance to "state your desire … anything! And it shall be yours!" It's a way for Doctor Doom to atone for the suffering he's caused them over the years.

Once Cap turns him down, Doctor Doom orders them to go. Cap notices that Spider-Woman is missing. He goes back into Doctor Doom's tower to find her. "If I'm not back in fifteen minutes, leave!"

Back inside, Cap discovers no apparent defenses, no alarms. He hears Klaw singing the classic American folk song "Home On the Range." When Cap turns the corner, there's the funniest panel in the whole twelve-issue series.

A very relaxed, shirtless, maskless Doctor Doom sits comfortably in his favorite chair, feet up on a table. Pictures of his mother are on the wall. It's made even funnier when Klaw says "Oops!" as Cap discovers them.

It's a fascinating new development for Doctor Doom's personality. He spent so much time in this series lusting for

power and trying several times to achieve it that, once he finally gets his wish, he's relaxing like a dad coming home from work after a hard day. Shooter has taken Doctor Doom on quite a journey.

Cap says Spider-Woman is missing. Doom orders Klaw to find her. Klaw searches the tower and gets tangled in one of Spider-Woman's webs. Spider-Woman grabs the trapped Klaw and the parasitic energy that inhabited her body is transferred to Doctor Doom's new friend.

Commenting on the portraits of his mother on the wall, Cap discovers that Doctor Doom is going to use his newfound powers for family. He's going to liberate his mother's "spirit essence" from the demon Mephisto.

Shooter has opened the door here for a future storyline that he or another writer can pick up and run with. Doctor Doom going after another classic Marvel villain to rescue his mother's spirit is a story that's just waiting to be told.

Cap thinks Doctor Doom looks "pretty normal to me." Doom explains that he's keeping his power contained, "lest an inadvertent flick of my finger should destroy a solar system or wipe out a galactic civilization."

Klaw returns, telling Cap that Spider-Woman is out in the hall. After Cap is gone, Klaw asks what's going on. Doom replies cryptically, "The inevitable, I fear."

Xavier senses that something is troubling Captain America.

As the group leaves Doom's tower, Cap asks Xavier to summon Colossus because they all need to make a decision "which affects all of us, and perhaps the entire universe."

Just where is Colossus? He's in a "glen near Zsaji's village" making out with the alien healer. A shirtless Colossus is summoned by Xavier, but Colossus tells him to "go away!" Xavier invokes the phrase "code red command," and Colossus realizes he must go. He promises Szaji that he'll come back: "I love you more than anything."

At Doombase, Cap lays it out. Doctor Doom's new power "rightfully belongs to no man." They must stop Doctor Doom. Everyone stands with Cap. Even Xavier and the X-Men sign on.

Cap warns, prophetically, that "if we do decide to confront Doom, it's possible that we might be annihilated by a bolt from the blue!"

Just as Cap predicted, the issue ends with a full-page splash of the group being annihilated by a bolt from the blue!

Ed Catto

"I was finishing up college when *Secret Wars* came out, and my life was about to change drastically. I remember being astonished at the some of the changes Secret Wars brought to the Marvel Universe and to my favorite characters. Before that, I always assumed that the characters' lives would have a more clearly defined, and predicable, trajectory. As usual, comics gave me a preview of real life."

Peter Sanderson

"Ever since then, Marvel and DC have been trying to repeat the success of *Secret Wars* by doing companywide crossover series that 'Will Change' the DC or Marvel Universe 'forever!' (or so they claim). These are now known as Event Comics."

"*Secret Wars* was—essentially—entirely motivated by a desire to sell action figures. But as a weird side effect, it's also a damn good story."
("The 11 Biggest Comic Book Events Ever" by Alex Zalben, MTV News, March 10, 2011)

Jim Shooter
"We've never seen them in a situation like this before. Never! And therefore, we'll see things emerging in them—fears, hopes, feelings, doubts—that usually remain hidden. And they'll all be changed by this experience for all time. How could they not be?"
(*Marvel Age* #20, November 1984)

14

Marvel Super Heroes Secret Wars #12

"… Nothing To Fear…"
Writer: Jim Shooter
Penciler: Mike Zeck
Inkers: John Beatty
Letterer: Joe Rosen
Colorist: Christie Scheele
Editor: Tom DeFalco
Cover by Mike Zeck

"Twenty-one lie dead here. Twenty-one heroes blown to pieces by a bolt from the blue."

Picking up mere seconds after the previous issue's power blast from Doctor Doom supposedly killed all the heroes, Captain America's broken shield lies in the rubble. Who wouldn't turn the page?

MARVEL®
© 1984 MARVEL COMICS GROUP
$1.00
12
APR
02475
APPROVED BY THE COMICS CODE AUTHORITY
#12 IN A TWELVE-ISSUE LIMITED SERIES
MARVEL SUPER HEROES™
SECRET WARS™
AFTER THE BIG BANG!

Thus begins the final issue of the series. It's a story so big that this is double-sized with a $1.00 cover price.

Hundreds of miles away, deep inside the Tower of Doom, the "author of the carnage" Doctor Doom has worn himself out. He draws his Beyonder powers back inside to "seal it up safely within the depths of my being."

With the power contained, Doctor Doom goes back to relaxing in the 1970s space-age bowl chair luxury of his "den," insisting that the heroes are dead: "they must be dead!"

Meanwhile, that chunk of Denver suburb is on its way to Earth, thanks to the power of Molecule Man. The villains relax in Volcana's "modest apartment." But the "exquisite Enchantress" has locked herself in the apartment's bathroom and draws a warm bath. But it's not for her. She calls forth a water elemental from the tub, demanding to know about the Beyonder.

The elemental responds with a two-page recap of the entire series. But Enchantress wants something else.

She applies extreme stress to the elemental: Is the Beyonder really dead? The shocking answer is that not only is the Beyonder still alive, he's very close to Doctor Doom. The Beyonder is "awaiting an opportunity—a moment of vulnerability."

After doing some quick calculations, Doctor Octopus has revealed that even if they're going in the right direction, "it'd take us a billion lifetimes to make the trip" to Earth.

Molecule Man claims he can get them home in a reasonable amount of time. While the villains argue, Enchantress lures Volcana out of the house to "a nearby glen." It's time for Volcana to make good on the promise she made to Enchantress back in issue #7.

Enchantress needs to teleport to Asgard to warn about the Beyonder. She needs more power and wants to use Volcana's life-force as a battery. It will kill Volcana, but she made "a mystic covenant" with Enchantress. It's binding.

Doctor Octopus's disagreement with Molecule Man gets out of hand quickly and devolves into a Marvel-style punch-out. It ends when the Lizard points out that "the witch-woman hass taken" Volcana. The Lizard and Molecule Man arrive in time to save Volcana from an energy-sucking death. Enchantress escapes via teleportation, inadvertently taking the Lizard to Battleworld with her. Oops.

Unperturbed, the Lizard still fights Enchantress, slashing her face with his gator-like claws. In response, she blasts him, ripping "away the life-force of a lower creature." The Lizard's life-force may give Enchantress the power boost she needs to teleport to Asgard.

Now that Klaw has been empowered by the mysterious energy that transferred from Spider-Woman, he sneaks up on the dozing Doctor Doom for some as-yet-unknown purpose. Doctor Doom awakens before Klaw can act.

Klaw, a self-described "master of sound," uses 3D images from "solidified sound-energy" to act out a little scenario about how Doctor Doom's new powers might've accidentally revived the heroes.

It's an interesting story choice to shift away from the heroes actively trying to revive themselves and to have that part told verbally. It gives Shooter a chance to focus on Doctor Doom and to have Klaw's story increase the stress and paranoia on the self-absorbed doctor.

Throughout the series, Doctor Doom has been hyper-confident and arrogant, with an answer and a plan for everything. Now, he's rattled because he doesn't really know if the heroes are dead or if he should believe Klaw.

As Klaw tells it, Zsaji the healer might've rushed to the scene of the heroes' destruction, maximized her healing power, and used the last of her own life-force to revive "the body of her lover Colossus." Drained of her healing force, "she dies in his arms. He weeps."

Colossus then takes the body of Reed Richards and using "the fortress's medical chambers" restores him to life. Reed would then take over and use "the alien technology of the fortress to invent and build a massive cell-regeneration device." With such technology, Reed would be able to bring back to life all of the dead heroes.

Of course, that's the way Klaw said it might happen, if Doctor Doom had inadvertently helped things along. Doctor Doom claims he killed them and that they are still dead. He says Klaw's "mad scenario is sheer nonsense!" Klaw still pushes his mad scenario and encourages Doom to turn on his new power and use his "godlike omniscience" to check on the heroes.

An angry Doctor Doom refuses. Every time he uses the new powers, he "grows weary" and falls asleep. Yet, "How many times in the past have I thought Reed Richards was dead?"

As if to answer Doctor Doom's doubts, here comes a dynamic splash page of Mjolnir, Thor's hammer, crashing through the tower. It's definitive proof that the heroes are alive. Doctor Doom "must let the power rise" after all. Unfortunately, given the high levels of his anger, frustration, and anxiety, Doctor Doom doesn't think he can control it.

And that's when Klaw's plan kicks into high gear. He offers to destroy the heroes once and for all on Doctor Doom's behalf. All Doctor Doom has to do is transfer some of his new power to Klaw. Doctor Doom gives Klaw "an infinitesimal micro-fraction" of his strength. It's "enough to blacken ten thousand suns," and it's far more than Klaw needs to slay the heroes.

What of Doctor Doom, then? He's going to struggle to contain the power he has left, and that means he has to lie down "and compose myself!" Meanwhile, Cap leads the revived heroes in an all-out assault on the Tower of Doom.

Before they can get inside the Tower of Doom, Klaw unleashes his newly acquired power by creating a kaiju-sized monster, then reviving Ultron and creating a monster army to support him.

Shooter sent all the other villains off to Earth in Volcana's apartment in the Denver suburb. With them out of the way, Shooter mixes it up by bringing in brand-new villains and tying them into Doctor Doom's new powers. This creates an opportunity for a different kind of battle that shows off some of that power.

And since the monsters have been created by Klaw channeling Doom's power, they are a little bit goofy as well as dangerous.

This leads to a double-page spread of fun Kirby-inspired monsters. It's action in the Mighty Marvel Manner as the heroes

are now fighting this new set of villains. Ben discovers he has the power to morph back into the Thing seemingly at will. Hulk smashes Ultron but not enough to avoid suffering a Hulk-sized leg injury. When a team-up of heroes can't bring down the robot, Wasp flies inside and pulls out his wiring. Ultron short-circuits, and another powerful villain is destroyed from the inside.

Cap bypasses Klaw, who now refers to himself as "Klaw the Mighty." Inside the Tower of Doom, Cap confronts Doctor Doom. But he isn't preparing for battle. He's totally relaxed, feet up, and enjoying a refreshing beverage.

With a cry of "Die, Avenger!" Doctor Doom blasts Cap. There's little time for Doctor Doom to enjoy the moment, as Cap is quickly revived and ready for battle again. Doctor Doom blasts him again. Cap dies and is again revived. This time, Doctor Doom crumbles without contact from Cap.

Now that little bit of energy—that "shimmering radiance"—that floated from Hulk to Spider-Woman to Klaw reveals itself to be the no-longer-weakened Beyonder. He's strong enough now to reclaim his power from Doctor Doom!

While begging Doctor Doom for forgiveness, Klaw explains that the Beyonder used "my guile, my wits, my cunning" to engineer stealing the power back from Doctor Doom.

The Beyonder changes Doctor Doom back to "as you were before!" Naturally, the first thing Klaw is concerned about is that Doctor Doom's perfect new face will be back to what it was. It feels like Klaw has a crush on his "master," and the two have been living like sitcom roommates. Before any more can be revealed, Klaw, Doctor Doom, and the Beyonder vanish in a blast of energy.

Just like that, it's over. A sequel had already been announced, so it feels like the Beyonder will return.

Also, it's Marvel Comics so everybody comes back eventually.

And thus begins the longest coda and goodbye sequence in comics.

Cap returns to the others, who have been waiting patiently outside the Tower of Doom after defeating Klaw's creatures from several pages earlier. They have important business to take care of back at Doombase: Zsaji's American-style funeral. A bereft Colossus refuses to leave his beloved's gravesite while "Jah-nee" doesn't seem to be bothered and never says a final goodbye.

Once that's all taken care of, Reed heads to the lab to find a way to get everyone back to Earth.

Spider-Man discovers he might've used the wrong machine to make his new black suit. Hulk gets a brace and a crutch for his injured leg. Hawkeye wants to make some high-powered arrows in case Hulk reverts to his primitive form. The Lizard is back in his human form. Lockheed finally returns, now paired with a dragon partner.

As an example of changes coming out of *Secret Wars,* the absence of Lockheed since issue #1 will eventually be explained in a separate storyline. Lockheed's dragon partner will also have a separate storyline as well by kaiju-ing over Tokyo.

According to Reed, the heroes are "experiencing an after-effect of the battle against Doom! The planet itself seems to have been charged with residual energy which seems to respond to strong desire, or force of will!"

Hearing this, Cap slips away to a table where he lays down his broken shield along with the little bits and pieces that were broken off earlier. Using "force of will … or sheer desire…" his shield is restored to its original perfect form. It's an incredibly joyful panel as the usually serious Cap gets back his greatest accessory.

Meanwhile, Reed's been busy. He has reverse-engineered the Beyonder's "construct" that teleported everyone to Battleworld. Once Reed beams everyone aboard, it'll teleport to Earth "with us in it."

Colossus initially wants to stay behind to mourn Zsaji. It takes Xavier's powers of persuasion to convince Colossus not to waste "the life she gave you." The new dragon inadvertently gets caught in the beam causing an "energy fluctuation." Reed hopes

this doesn't cause problems back on Earth, which feels like a future storyline.

She-Hulk casually announces that she's taking the Thing's place in the Fantastic Four. The Thing likes that he can change back into Ben Grimm at any time, and he wants to stay for a while to "do some thinkin'!"

As the final panel closes out the series, Ben sits on an alien rock, contemplating his future like a high school graduate.

The Marvel Age of Name-Calling

Enchantress calls Volcana a "sow."

The Marvel Age of Euphemisms

Wolverine accuses Lockheed of getting "some R and R with a local chippie."

Jim Shooter

"Mike [Zeck] and John [Beatty] were so patient with me, and with all the changes, corrections, and fussy details that *Secret Wars* requires, that they proved themselves true professionals, and possibly candidates for sainthood."
(*Marvel Age* #20, November 1984)

Milton Griepp

"The legacy of *Secret Wars* is just the idea that a comic universe is a tool that can be used in creating stories that encompass that whole universe. And that's something that hadn't been done up to that point."

15

Double the Size, Double the Headaches

Secret Wars #12 is legendary because the published issue is not the issue that was originally finished. On the eve of the deadline, Jim Shooter decided that the issue was "unprintable."

Tom DeFalco's assistant editor on *Secret Wars* was Eliot R. Brown, a fixture of the famous bullpen. He breaks down what happened:

> "I'm not sure what the problem was, but Jim wanted the book to be redrawn. It might've been half the book. Marvel rented a penthouse suite at a hotel around the corner from the Marvel offices. This was very last minute and everybody

who was available went in. It was a small crew. They were paid 'hazardous duty pay.' We also got a nice meal and that was fun because freelancers march on their stomach.

Mike Zeck was there, watching a football game and drawing whatever needed to be drawn. Keith Williams and Art Nichols were inkers. Christie Scheele the colorist was there. Letterer Jack Morelli. Tom DeFalco. Jim was there for some of the time, too.

We also did it in pieces, often one panel at a time, a half-page here, and so on. All out of order. Tom was in charge of keeping track of the continuity so everything fit.

This is when the bullpen shines. We have a task in front of us and it just gets done. We all knew we were doing something special.

I never did see the finished issue before it left the office. And I wish I'd managed to get photocopies of the original version. I just wasn't thinking ahead."

16

The End of the *Secret Wars*

"Let's be honest. *Secret Wars* was crap, right? But did it sell?" (Carol Kalish, Marvel's Direct Sales Manager, 1980s)

What are the most important comics in the Marvel Universe?

Surely, there's *Amazing Fantasy* #15 with the first appearance of Spider-Man near the top of the list. *Fantastic Four* #1, the beginning of the epic family story by Stan Lee and Jack Kirby, certainly. *The Avengers* #4 featuring the return of Captain America by Stan and Jack would be on that list as well.

Jumping ahead to 1984, Marvel's *Secret Wars* had not one but two important issues during its twelve-issue run, including the first appearance of Spider-Man's new black costume.

That's only part of the legacy of Marvel's *Secret Wars.*

The series that started to put multiple characters into

multiple fight scenarios in order to sell toys. It turned out to be incredibly successful and a lot of fun.

For many fans, it was their *Star Wars.* For others, it was a dream come true—the ultimate team-up of Marvel characters. For Shooter, he was building on the legacy of Stan and Jack and the promise of the Marvel Universe.

Some older fans were critical of the series, but sales figures won that argument. An immediate and more complicated crossover sequel was greenlit while *Secret Wars* was still being published.

Marvel published other subsequent *Secret Wars* series over the years. The new black Spider-Man costume became a separate character. The Beyonder would continue to pop up in various titles, as would Battleworld. Even Titania and Volcana would continue as villains in the Marvel Universe.

Marvel collected all twelve issues of *Secret Wars* into a thick trade paperback that's still in print today, more than 40 years after the original run. Fans new and old can continue to discover the ultimate super-hero team-up that Shooter, Zeck, Beatty, and others brought to four-color life.

The name *Secret Wars* became a legitimate brand. It's a name as familiar to the industry as Spider-Man and The Avengers. It's become synonymous with a blockbuster event and invoking the name now brings speculation about who will be impacted next in the Marvel Universe.

According to Ed Catto, comics historian and editor of *Retro Fan* magazine, "*Secret Wars* reinforced the important, unrelenting relationship between publishing and merchandising. It's more than just buying the published comic books. *Secret Wars* led the way, and the symbiotic merchandising continues to this day."

The writer Fabian Nicieza, who was also once Marvel's Advertising Manager, said: "The book sold so well that everything afterwards was measured by its standards. As one of the people who, soon afterwards, was responsible for promoting our books to increase their sales, that was a very daunting bar that *Secret Wars* had set."

Marvel still touted the success of *Secret Wars* years after the original release. In a letter dated April 1, 1987, Marvel's James Sokolowski wrote to Gil Brechtel at Graham News Company in Kenner, LA, about the sales success of *Secret Wars*. It says: "in the May 1984 issue of *The Amazing Spider-Man* everyone's favorite wall-crawler traded in his traditional 'red and blue' skivvies for the dramatic 'black and white' costume he wears today. On a national basis, sales skyrocketed! We cut the May '84 print order 1.6% and unit sales went up 76.2%. National sell-through shot up 34 points, from 43% (April '84) to 77% (May '84)."

Writer and comics historian John Jackson Miller adds, "While I think *Secret Wars* drove a lot of attention, the every-title aspect of it proved burdensome for creators most other times it was repeated—and, in many cases, for readers (and especially their wallets)."

In January 1985 (cover dated April 1985), DC Comics started publishing its own twelve-issue mini-series event, *Crisis On Infinite Earths*. The crossover series had been in development since 1981 when writer Marv Wolfman (a former Marvel editor) pitched the idea. "*Secret Wars* was being done to promote a toy line while *Crisis* was created to help revamp the DCU. We weren't going for the same audience. *Crisis* and *Secret Wars* were apples and oranges."

Paul Levitz, the former president and publisher of DC Comics, noted: "I think *Secret Wars* proved that you could do it as command performance rather than as 'shaking a universe.' The challenge for *Crisis* was that we felt in order to have any credibility for it to matter we really had to change stuff. *Secret Wars* showed that you didn't. You can put the thing together where what you did within it mattered because you said they mattered. And Marvel did an elegant job with that."

Ray Wagner, the Mattel executive who initiated the deal with Marvel for what would become *Secret Wars*, left the company in 1983, before the first comic book was published. He formed his own consulting firm and died suddenly in 1985 at the age of 53.

Jim Shooter was fired from Marvel on April 15, 1987. He would go on to found at least three subsequent comic book companies with varying degrees of success. He died on June 30, 2025. In his obituary for Shooter in *The Hollywood Reporter*, Borys Kit wrote, "He instituted the concept of publishing crossover events, a companywide initiative that saw one main story play out and influence many of the other titles coming out for months on end. *Secret Wars* was a massive publishing success."

Perhaps comics historian and former Marvel freelancer Peter Sanderson sums it up best: "The legacy of *Secret Wars* is best demonstrated by the fact that Marvel Studios is doing a movie titled *Avengers: Secret Wars*, which will come out in December 2027. It's supposed to star Doctor Doom and a wide range of super heroes. It's too bad that Jim Shooter did not live to attend its premiere."

Dave Olbrich

"Marvel and DC have been working furiously for more than 40 years to duplicate the success of *Secret Wars*, with predictably mixed results."

Rob Liefeld

"The original [*Secret Wars*] is heralded, beloved, celebrated. It's a seminal event, and changed the course of comic books. It introduced the blockbuster crossover. So much of this is the byproduct of the sheer genius of Jim Shooter."

("Robservations" podcast, June 5, 2025)

ILLUSTRATIONS

SPECIAL THANKS TO THE AUTHOR'S BULLPEN

Pat Brosseau is an Eisner-nominated comic book letterer who has worked for every major comic book company and considers BATHROOOOM to be his favorite sound effect.

Eliot R. Brown worked for Marvel Comics from 1979 to 1995, including a stint as Tom DeFalco's assistant editor during *Secret Wars.*

Pop culture historian **Ed Catto** is the editor of *RetroFan,* a magazine specializing in pop culture.

Barry Dutter is a former Marvel editor and freelance writer. He now buys and sells comic collections online.

Writer **Danny Fingeroth** was the editor of the *Spider-Man* comics before, during, and after *Secret Wars.* He is the author of *A Marvelous Life: The Amazing Story of Stan Lee* and *Jack Ruby: The Many Faces of Oswald's Assassin.*

Milton Griepp (icv2.com) was the co-founder and president of Capital City Distribution and is now the CEO of ICV2 which covers the business of geek culture.

Paul Levitz is the former President and Publisher of DC Comics. Both he and Jim Shooter wrote *Legion of Super-Heroes* stories at DC and played poker together.

Writer **John Jackson Miller** is the former editor of *Comics Retailer*, the founder of the Comichron website that tracks comic book circulation statistics, and has written best-selling novels in the Star Wars, Star Trek, and Batman universes.

Novelist **Fabian Nicieza** (*Suburban Dicks, The Self-Made Widow*) was also once Marvel's Advertising Manager.

Dave Olbrich was the editor of *Amazing Heroes* in 1984. He was Publisher and co-founder of Malibu Comics, the launch Publisher of Image Comics, a co-founder of the Ultraverse and is the Marketing, and Publications Editor for the San Diego Comic Convention.

Steve Saffel was Assistant Promotions Manager at Marvel Comics in 1984. He since worked in executive capacities at Del Rey Books and Titan Books and wrote the biography *Joe Simon: My Life in Comics.*

Comics historian **Peter Sanderson** (substack.com/@petersanderson1) was a freelance researcher for Marvel Comics in 1984, working on *The Official Handbook of the Marvel Universe*. He writes the *Sanderson On Comics* Substack.

Bob Wayne is a former Texas comics retailer who was later DC Comics' Senior Vice President of Sales.

Marv Wolfman has been an award-winning writer and editor for both Marvel Comics and DC Comics. He may be best known for his work on *Tomb of Dracula* for Marvel, *Teen Titans* for DC, and the event series *Crisis On Infinite Earths*.

ABOUT THE AUTHOR

Tom K. Mason is an Emmy-winning television writer with credits as writer, story editor, or head writer on more than 600 episodes of childrens' entertainment. As a co-founder of Malibu Comics, he edited more than 1,000 comics and wrote close to 100 of them. He was a founding editor of Bravura, the comic book imprint created by Howard Chaykin, Walter Simonson, Jim Starlin and others. He was also a co-founder of the superhero universe Ultraverse. He recently wrote a *Lilo & Stitch* graphic novel for TokyoPop, and has written more than 70 books for children.

MARVEL AGE OF COMICS

Explore the series!

www.bloomsbury.com/marvel-books

Doctor Strange: A Decade of Dark Magic
by Stuart Moore

The story of one of Marvel's most bizarre, otherworldly heroes, beginning with his creation at the hands of Stan Lee and artist/plotter Steve Ditko, and discussed against the backdrop of one of the most turbulent decades in American history.

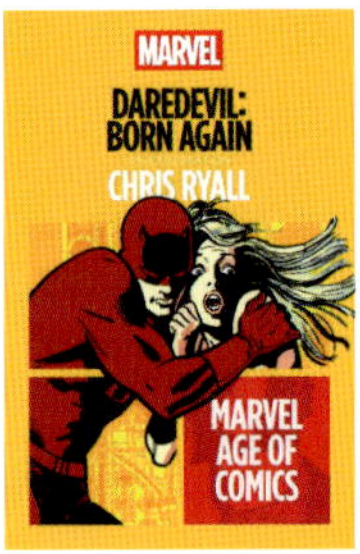

Daredevil: Born Again
by Chris Ryall

A smart, meticulous look into the compelling and original storyline of *Daredevil: Born Again*, its gorgeous and unique artwork, and its overall influence in the decades since its release.

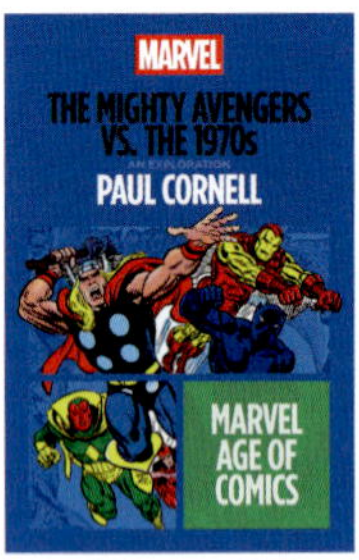

The Mighty Avengers vs. the 1970s
by Paul Cornell

The Avengers was **the** comic book of the 1970s. From Civil Rights to Women's Lib, battles for the soul of America became battles between super heroes.

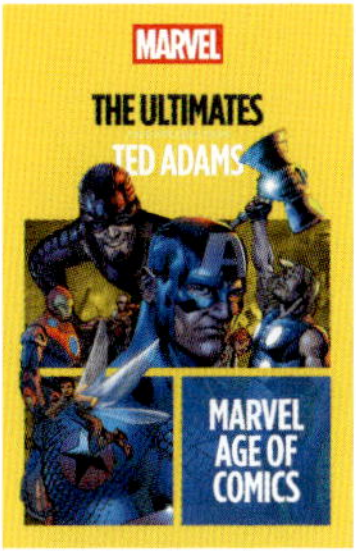

The Ultimates
by Ted Adams

The 1990s and early 2000s were a time of intense change and experimentation for Marvel Comics. Out of this emerged *The Ultimates*—a comic which would have an explosive impact on Marvel and the broader pop culture landscape.

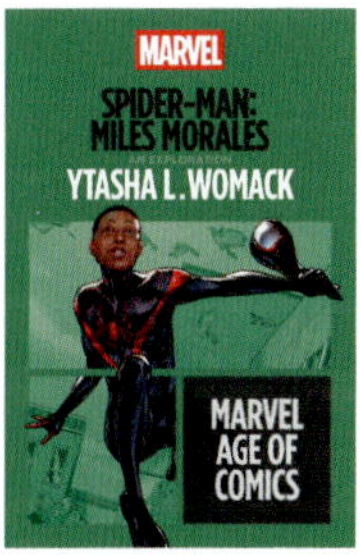

Spider-Man: Miles Morales
by Ytasha L. Womack

A look at the hugely successful reimagining of one of the most popular super hero characters of all time.

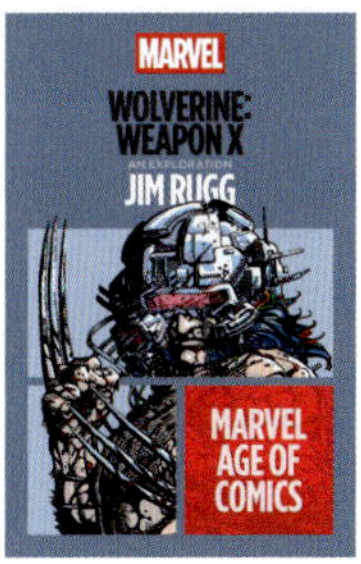

Wolverine: Weapon X
by Jim Rugg

A deep-dive into one of Marvel's most experimental and brutal comics, and what many consider to be **the** definitive Wolverine story.

Marvel Explodes: From Bullpen to Big Business
by Paul Levitz

A comics industry insider looks at the growth of Marvel from 1967 to 1975, the years in which it established its greatness.

Misty Knight: Iconic and Bionic
by Angélique Roché

Marvel's first Black woman super hero, Misty Knight broke down stereotypes and became one of the backbone characters of the Marvel Universe.